THE ART OF WAR
ART OF TENNIS

孫子兵法

SKY KIM

Coach Sky Kim was born on September 3, 1984 in Seoul, South Korea. He started playing tennis at the age of 7 and moved to the United States with his family to play tennis at the age of 8. In the U.S. he reached the top 5 in every age division and received a full scholarship to the IMG Tennis Academy, also known as the Nick Bollettieri Tennis Academy. He has trained with Tommy Haas, Maria Sharapova, Venus and Serena Williams, Monica Seles, Max Mirnyi, Parul-Henri Mathieu, Xavier Malisse, Jalena Jankovic, Daniella Hantuchova, Mariana Lucic, and many other top pros. He reached a top ATP ranking of #481, but his pro career was stopped short by a childhood injury that was not tennis-related. As a coach, he has sent several players to Division 1 colleges in the U.S. He has also worked with pro players in South Korea and traveled with top junior players from his homeland. He is currently the CEO of Road to Pro and the inventor of the Tennis Swing Training System.

Author

Sky Kim
Road to Pro, Inc.
info@roadtoprotennis.com
www.roadtoprotennis.com

Design

Solid Creact
www.solidcreact.com

Copyright 2017 Road to Pro, Inc. All Rights Reserved.

THE ART OF WAR: ART OF TENNIS

孫子兵法

By Sky Kim

Acknowledgments

Special thanks to:

Jimmy Arias who introduced me to the
concept of playing strategic tennis.

Nick Bollettieri for believing in my tennis.

My beautiful and understanding wife Yeo Jin,
her parents, my sister-in-law Reena,
and my son Leo.

My parents for giving me the opportunity to
play this awesome sport and disciplining me
the way they have.

My sister and my parents for all the sacrifices
they made for me.

My grandfather and artist Woo Young Ko
for introducing me to all the stories of
ancient warfare.

And all the people I've met in my life.

PROLOGUE

In a sense, I've played tennis professionally for my entire life. I was never allowed to play tennis for recreational purposes. My family came to the United States just so I could become a professional tennis player. I didn't have a choice when I was young. Luckily, I loved tennis, but I hated competing in tennis. It was weird because I loved competing in everything but tennis. If I could have developed, at an early age, a better understanding of tennis and better mindset to prepare myself for the challenges ahead, I would have enjoyed the competition and loved tennis even more. Wishing that I could write to myself, my friends, and my family in the past, I am writing this book in hopes of helping the parents, coaches, and players to better prepare for and enjoy the short—but seemingly endless—years that they will be investing their time in tennis through my own experiences and experiences of others around me.

INTRODUCTION

Relationship between War and Tennis

Art of War: Art of Tennis is about the relationship between warfare/survival and tennis. The mentality, preparations, strategies, and tactics are very closely related to warfare and survival tactics. As I considered how to explain the difficulties and answer the unanswered questions related to competitive tennis, I arrived at the idea of comparing it to preparing for war and fighting battles. While there have been previous comparisons of sports to warfare, to my knowledge, it has never been done specifically for tennis.

The Art of War by Sun Tzu

Art of Tennis is based on the philosophy described more than 2,000 years ago by renowned Chinese war strategist Sun Tzu in his book *The Art of War*. *The Art of War* was written to help govern a nation politically, economically, and militarily. Aside from his legacy as the author of *The Art of War*, Sun Tzu is revered in Chinese and Asian culture as a legendary historical figure. There were 82 chapters in the original book, but later versions were stripped down to 13 chapters. There are similar aspects in some chapters, and every chapter is closely related to others in some way. In this book, I'm using paraphrased passages from *The Art of War* to help describe the similarities between war and tennis.

Understanding Tennis

It's easy to see why people with competitive personalities and minds enjoy tennis. The competitive nature of the sport and the unforgiving point system require a significant amount of self-management and self-control. *Art of Tennis* also helps explain the roles of parents, coaches, and players by comparing the team to a nation. The literal translation of *The Art of War* is very detailed but broad, abstract but realistic, complex but simple, and exciting but boring. *Art of Tennis* uses some of the ideas in *The Art of War* as jumping-off points for helping people understand and view tennis in a different way.

Warfare is closely related to politics and economics – financial support

The foremost aspect Sun Tzu has written about warfare is the importance of the nation's economic strength to deploy an army of 100,000 men in the Strategy/Operations chapter. The success or failure of an army can often be determined by the nation's size, resources, and supplies. As Sun Tzu explains, "Only after comparing and analyzing the resources and supplies, can the calculation be made to forecast a victory." The relevance to tennis is in the financial backing parents can provide. With very limited financial resources from the parents, the player will not go far. Generally speaking, the better the funds are managed, the higher the chances of success. The more battles the nation fights, the faster the resources and supplies are depleted. Parents should be careful of how they manage their financial assets.

War is not for amusement – seriousness in professional and top junior level tennis

Sun Tzu was an expert in warfare, and people may think that he was a war-inclined person, but it was rather the opposite. He wrote *The Art of War* to advocate for a cautious and strategic approach when war was unavoidable. His goal was to win while minimizing casualties along the way. I'm writing this book with the same intentions as Sun Tzu. If you're already involved in tennis with the goal of reaching the professional level—whether you're a parent, coach, or player—it will help you prepare for the battles ahead. If your goal isn't to become a pro but play at a competitive level, then it will help you understand and approach tennis in a different way. I understand as well as Sun Tzu did that war, in the worst-case scenario, can lead to widespread destruction and the downfall of a nation. To paraphrase a passage from *The Art of War*, a perished nation cannot be rebuilt and the dead cannot be revived. The stories of the victorious champions are the ones people love to hear, but there are countless untold stories of people who have tried and failed and are left broken. Do not take competitive tennis lightly. When you look at countries that are thriving at the top of the tennis world, most of the time, having fun is not high on their list of priorities. It is always hard work, but if you do a few things right early in your career, you'll be able to have plenty of fun later on.

The virtues of the king – parents

When a king reigns over a nation with care and works to unify the nation, the people will not be afraid to sacrifice and will follow the king's guidance. If the morals of the king are not set properly, the king's end will be miserable. This explains how important the king's roles are for a nation. The parents play a vital role in the success of a player. This does not mean that the parents as kings should interfere with every little detail. The role of a king is different from that of a tactical general (coach) or a combat general (player). Sun Tzu knew the significance of war, but he also knew that using troops unwisely would simply make them tired and reduce their strength. He knew that if the troops' fighting spirit was diminished, the performance of the entire military unit would be affected. He frequently stressed how important it was not to waste any resources or supplies. This can apply to the coaches and players as the generals and troops in warfare. The parents must be careful not to disrespect the coach or diminish the fighting spirit of the player.

Views of warfare – accurate views of the team

Sun Tzu was not against war, nor did he think it was wrong, but he advised viewing it clearly and accurately since war was inevitable. Parents, coaches, and players must be able to judge situations clearly and play the correct roles in order for the team to perform efficiently. This book will help parents, coaches, and players view tennis clearly as a whole. Sun Tzu's *The Art of War*, which was written over 2,000 years ago, not only covered the wisdom of warfare, but it offered deep insights into people's psychology. The original book can be thought of as a "Bible to Victory" rather than as a guide to warfare alone.

Bible to Victory – more than an aggressive mindset

The teachings in *The Art of War* acknowledge the importance of survival. Not only is it important to win a battle; the book also talks about how to be victorious even without actually battling the enemies; how offense is second to defense; and the importance of "not losing" versus "winning at all costs." He also focuses on the importance of virtues of mentors, which are wisdom/wit (智), righteousness (仁), bravery (勇), faith (信), and discipline (嚴). *The Art of War* is read and praised by some of the most renowned leaders like Bill Gates, Napoléon Bonaparte, and Chairman Mao for being a political science handbook. It is also recommended for all United States military intelligence personnel and is required reading for all CIA officers.

The complexity of *The Art of War*

The original phrases from *The Art of War* are very difficult to explain because of the book's emphasis on trickery and misdirection. The concepts of "what is seen can't be believed," "trick your enemies," "regular warfare and unconventional warfare," and "surprise attacks and frontal attacks" are all meshed into the fundamentals. The basis of warfare can be described as deception, but one must understand that within the deception, it is important to know what does change and what does not. It is difficult to grasp how this is all related to tennis when the game is played inside a court with lines and a net between the two players (singles). But since there are certain limits to the grounds on which the game is played that do not change, it will be fairly easy to understand. And once these concepts are fully understood, tennis can be the most rewarding and fun game ever.

Breaking down the chapters

The first sections of the book will compare a team—consisting of parents, a coach, and a player—to a nation and analyze the roles and relationships among them.

The subsequent chapters will explore the art of developing a tennis player and how it is related to warfare, including the scoring system, preparations, strategy and tactics, deception, forms of offense and defense, adaptation, improvisation, fitness and endurance, mentality and cheating, and other aspects of tennis.

This is not a how-to book. It is intended to help people understand tennis differently, and it is inspired by many of the concepts and historical stories in *The Art of War*.

CONTENTS

Throughout the book, you will see two-part phrases separated by a long dash(–). In these phrases, the left portion is a paraphrase from *The Art of War* or *The Romance of the Three Kingdoms*, and the right portion represents similar ideas relating to tennis.

PROLOGUE

INTRO Comparison between war and tennis.

SECTION 1
Understanding the team before turning pro: one nation

I.	**Parents – king (君主) infinite love and support – governing a nation**	26
a)	Role as the king	26
b)	Resources and supplies – financial assets	27
c)	Two-faced king – single mind vs. two minds	28
d)	The tyrant or the gentle king? – extremely strict parents vs. extremely relaxed parents	28
e)	The ungrateful combat general (將軍) – financial pressure felt by young players	29
f)	Interferences or interests from the king – differences in coaching your own child/children and showing interest in their work	30
g)	Your general complaining to go to battle – tantrums on and off the court in tournaments	30
h)	Young warriors' minds when they go into battle – what are	31

	they thinking about when they play a match; or what do they need to think about; technique or strategy?	
i)	Taking a defeat gracefully – when your child loses in battle	32
j)	Surrendering to the enemy general – quitting or tanking a match (whining)	33
k)	Who will be the one punishing the general? – no excuse but need to hear what they have to say	33
l)	Stopping or interfering with the punishment – loss of respect and punishment unfinished	34
m)	Hiring the tactician (參謀) – hiring a coach	34
n)	Once the mightiest combat general of all the land – not all great players make great coaches	35
o)	Hiring the famous reluctant tactical general (三顧草廬) – hiring a stubborn but famous coach	36
p)	The loyal and sincere counsel (忠臣) and the treacherous counsel (奸臣) – what the king needs to hear and what the king wants to hear	37
q)	Listening to your tactical generals – guidance from your coach	37
r)	Combat general meets tactical general – when a new coach starts coaching your player	38
s)	Are more tactical generals better? – hiring multiple coaches for your player	38
t)	The foolish king controlling the army – parents coaching without solid tennis background	39
u)	The disrespectful, dirty, and shameless enemy combat general – handling cheaters	39
v)	The king going into the battlefield with the combat general – anxious parents and coaching during a match	40
w)	Giving gifts, throwing parties, or letting your generals relax – they are human	41
x)	Hiring an outside tactical general for a couple of battles – using an outside coach just for a couple of tournaments	42
y)	King to king – parents' views of other parents	42
z)	Hiring a drill sergeant (教官) – the lack of discipline, body balance, and endurance	42
aa)	Wounded generals – injuries and injury prevention	43

bb)	The great doctor (名醫) – more than rest, ice, compression, elevation	43
cc)	Base camp (基地) – choosing a tennis academy	44
dd)	Training camp (训练所) – sending the kids to academy by themselves	45
ee)	Good habits and lifestyle - learned from the parents' lifestyles	45
ff)	Successor to the throne (承繼)	45

II.	**Coaches – tactical generals (參謀 – advisor), the brains**	47
a)	Role of a tactical general – leader and supporter	48
b)	The experiences as a warrior and a king (?!) – trying to understand the coach	48
c)	The supporting act – it's not about you (coach), don't expect them to understand	49
d)	Talking to the king, the tactical general's superior – with class and dignity yet compassionate	49
e)	Price of lessons and services (給料) – price vs. respect	50
f)	The ultimate test of the king and the tactical general (諫言) – admonition/remonstration	50
g)	Sacrificing themselves as a tactical general or an advisor – the coaches should have a life too	51
h)	Tactical general asking for total control – ignoring the roles of the parents	52
i)	Keeping the king happy – relationship between the coach and the player	52
j)	Training the army without the supervision of the king – working hard to improve the player when the parents are not present on the court	52
k)	Gifts, rewards, and vacations from the king – not a privilege, do not expect them	53
l)	Talking to your combat general – similar to talking to your young self when you were the young warrior	53
m)	In the middle of the king and the combat general – the middle man: serious and polite to the king and a source of enjoyment for the combat generals	54
n)	Training and disciplining the young warrior – discipline vs. abuse	55

o)	Regulating the young warrior – compassionate vs. merciless	56
p)	Maturing combat general – staying knowledgeable and respected	57
q)	The perfect tactical general – over-confident coach	57
r)	Giving some space to the combat general - they need time to learn about themselves	58
s)	Zooming in and out of the battlefield – ability to see the technical, tactical, mental, and the overall flow of the game	58
t)	Leadership before going into war – leadership before going to tournaments	59
u)	Picking battles – choosing which pro and high-level junior tournaments to play	59
v)	Constantly checking the health of your generals – injury prevention and rehab training	60
w)	Disciplining your generals – teaching them correct and proper routines and having respect for others	60
x)	Recruiting or taking combat generals from other nations – taking players from other academies or coaches	61
y)	Base camp crumpled – fall of an academy	61
z)	Blank ammunition training – hitting with dead balls	61
aa)	Combat general to the new king – junior to pro; the difference between pro and amateur/juniors	62
bb)	Manipulation and anticipation – reading minds and actions from experience and calculations to act and react to the situations	62
III.	**Players - combat general (將軍 - general) and the platoons (小隊)**	64
a)	The role of the combat general – love for tennis and the competition	65
b)	The strong connection but inconsiderate king – player to parents relationship	65
c)	Talking to the king – your coach is your best bet to be a bridge of understanding	66
d)	Preparing for training and battle – not just a mindset; checking equipment and preparing supplies	66

e)	Outer appearance – the way people view you as a player	67
f)	The eyes of the tiger and killer instincts – confidence and training	68
g)	Expecting the unexpected: do as your drill sergeant tells you – fitness, rehab, and endurance training	68
h)	Training to the max and pushing beyond the limits – second wind	69
i)	Battling with fatigue and minor wounds – playing with soreness training and in matches	70
j)	Controlling emotions – expectations and expecting the worst	71
k)	Communication with the tactical general – bidirectional communication	71
l)	The mightiest and fiercest general of all the land, Lu Bu – players that don't listen and only believe in themselves	72
m)	Inevitable and under-prepared battles – not wanting to play tournaments and matches	72
n)	Into the battlefield with a knife instead of a gun – going into a match without confidence	73
o)	Nervousness before battles – sensitivity and feeling the pressure before matches and tournaments	73
p)	Into the battlefield – decisions in the match	74
q)	Staying focused in battle – concentration and self-talk	75
r)	Improvising on the battlefield – pre-calculations are not always correct	76
s)	Signs from the tactical general – signs from the coach or parents during a match	76
t)	Losing weapons in battle – losing the feel of a shot during a match	77
u)	The ultimate sin, surrendering to the enemy general – quitting or tanking a match	77
v)	Importance of not surrendering – player's no-surrender character	77
w)	Comeback victory – bigger the gap, the sweeter the victory	78
x)	The scolding king – dealing with angry and upset parents	78
y)	After the lost battle, it's not the end – analyzing and preparing for training with the coach after a loss	79 79

z)	Respecting other nations' generals – respecting the other players and their coaches	
aa)	Shameful and dishonorable tactics – bad line calls, cheating or mistakes?	79
bb)	Weapon of choice – equipment: rackets, strings, shoes, etc.	80
cc)	Everything matters – professionalism	81
dd)	Rest and resupplying – resting is training too	82
ee)	Friends outside of tennis – the best friends without all the jealousy and rivalry	82
ff)	I want to rule all the nations one day, be the king – becoming pro and working to be number 1	82

SECTION 2
Understanding the art of professional tennis

I.	**Initial calculations (計) – planning ahead**	87
a)	War decides the fate of life and death	88
b)	Five factors to understand before going into war	90
c)	Seven calculations to measure the team's capacity and abilities	92
d)	Strategy and tactics = deception	97
e)	The probability of victory	99
II.	**Waging war (作戰) – importance of finances and resources and maintaining morale on the road**	102
a)	Calculate the expenses	103
b)	Dragging on a match can lead to defeat	105
c)	Fitness training at the tournament	107
d)	The cost of traveling and training	108
e)	Rewards and prize money	111
III.	**Plan of attack (謀攻) – introduction to the overall strategy of attack**	112

a)	Win without fighting	113
b)	Besieging the enemy's castle – taking down a pusher/defensive player	116
c)	Rules of engagement	119
d)	Three things the king should not get involved in; generals' matters	121
e)	Five ways to victory	123
f)	If you know the enemy and know yourself, you need not fear the result of a hundred battles	125
IV.	**Disposition of the military (形) – players' tendencies, style of play, and base power**	**128**
a)	Neutralize your enemy	129
b)	"Way to fight out there" is not a compliment	134
c)	The road to complete victory	136
V.	**Form of power (勢) – strategical flexibility and shot selection**	**139**
a)	Know-how for executing the strategies	141
b)	Tactics that paralyze the senses	144
c)	Importance of momentum and quality of shot selection	146
d)	Baiting and counter-attacking	147
e)	Momentum is fed by shot selection	151
f)	Zoning in tennis	154
VI.	**Weaknesses and strengths (虛實)**	**155**
a)	Get there before the opponent (opponent's shots)	157
b)	The rules of military march (court positioning) and defensive measures (anticipation)	159
c)	Unwritten laws of offense and defense	161
d)	Concentration and dispersing the concentration	163
e)	Attack and defend against one's expectations	165
f)	Four ways to analyze the enemy's strengths and weaknesses	167
g)	Resembling the nature of water	170
VII.	**Military maneuvers (軍爭) – traveling for tournaments**	**172**

	a)	Easy route is the difficult route	173
	b)	Rushing to tournaments	175
	c)	Wind, forest, fire, and mountain – the natural environmental elements	177
	d)	Eye contact and signals from the coach	180
	e)	Governing one's spirits and energy to fight – biorhythm (治氣), mental toughness (治心), endurance (治力), circumstances (治變)	182
	f)	Forbidden actions while in battle	185
VIII.		**Variations and adaptations (九變) – changes in tactics and strategies**	187
	a)	The art of war of varying plans	188
	b)	Do not rely on the enemy's actions but rely on your readiness to counter their actions	190
	c)	Five dangerous faults of a general	192
IX.		**Movement of the army (行軍) – movement of the player and the team**	194
	a)	Tactics to attack according to the opponent's court positioning	195
	b)	Checking the players for injury and overall health	210
	c)	No man's land	211
	d)	33 movements of the enemy	212
	e)	Do not underestimate and do not be afraid	220
	f)	The coach/player relationship – not too close, not too distant	221
X.		**Terrain (地形) – zones of the court**	223
	a)	Attack zones of the court	224
	b)	Six types of faults leading to defeat	242
	c)	It is not a matter of who is right or wrong	244
	d)	Warmhearted but being strict to the player	246
	e)	Know thyself, know thy enemy, and know the environment	247

XI.	**Nine battlegrounds** (九地) **– scoring system and point management**	249
a)	The nine grounds and point management	251
b)	Attacking what the opponent holds dear	255
c)	Managing the players to keep the right mindset when traveling	257
d)	Like the Shuai-jan, the snake	260
e)	Too much information for the players	262
f)	Different psychological states of the players by points	264
g)	Importance of point management	269
h)	Calmness of a maiden and rapidity of a running hare	271
XII.	**Attacking with fire** (火攻) **– anger management**	273
a)	Handling different types of fire	274
b)	Possible developments with fire attacks	277
c)	A kingdom that has once been destroyed can never come again into being	280
XIII.	**Intelligence and espionage** (用間)	282
a)	Getting information from others	283
b)	Information from different types of people	286
c)	Befriending other nations' officers and spies	290

EPILOGUE 293

THE ART OF WAR
ART OF TENNIS
孫子兵法

SECTION 1

Understanding the Team Before Turning Pro – One Nation

Chapter 1 is about the relationships and roles required to build a strong nation. This section was written to help clarify the roles of parents, coaches, and players, to explain each team member's duties and the need for mutual respect for everyone involved. This chapter is inspired by stories in *The Art of War*, as well as the Three Kingdoms (三國志) period in Chinese history and the beginning of the Han dynasty (楚漢志), which was founded by its first emperor, Liu Bang.

I.

PARENTS = KING (君主), INFINITE LOVE AND SUPPORT – GOVERNING A NATION

When parents pull up a folding chair next to the court and observe the coach as he trains their child, what does that remind you of? The king enjoying his military might and watching his troops train?

Role as the king

More parents are starting to get educated on the proper way to parent a tennis player, but I still don't think they realize how important their job is as the king. Every role is important, but some are more important than others. Even though some may disagree with the idea of viewing parents as kings and suggest that the focus should be on the player, there are many similarities between raising a tennis player and building a nation. Just because their children are the ones that are battling it out on the court, that doesn't mean the role of the king isn't important to the team. Kings play a vital role in building a strong nation and also need to know when to step down and give the throne to their young warrior when he or she is mature enough. The best tennis parents are graceful and wise but also fierce leaders. The combat general does not respect the king for his knowledge of war; he relies on the king for overall guidance in life and fundamental beliefs. Remember, your child does not have teammates as in other sports. It's him/her versus the world. Every player he or she meets at a tournament is a potential enemy. Even combat generals in ancient times had friends, but there were multiple generals for a nation (college), and there were inevitably some trust issues within the nation. You are the only one that the child can trust at all times. Show them that you care and that you are always on their side.

Resources and supplies – financial assets

A nation that does not have stable financial assets cannot afford to go to war against other nations. It's costly and there is no guarantee of winning. Any potential spoils of war must be calculated to see if the battle is worth fighting. In the lower levels of professional tennis, there is very little money to be made. In the first chapters of *The Art of War*, Sun Tzu explains the importance of the nation's economic strength to deploy an army of 100,000 men in the Strategy/Operations chapter. The success or failure of an army can often be determined by the nation's size, resources, and supplies. As Sun Tzu explains, "Only after comparing and analyzing the resources and supplies, can the calculation be made to forecast a victory." In tennis, this can be compared to the level of financial backing parents can provide. With limited financial support from the parents, the player will not go far. Generally speaking, the better the funds are managed, the higher the player's chances of success. The more battles the nation fights, the faster the resources and supplies are depleted. Parents should be careful about how they manage their financial assets.

Two-faced king – single mind vs. two minds

The king is one person, but the role of king in tennis is shared by mother and father. The difficult part about this is that mother and father can have different goals for their child. For example, one might want their child to focus on academics and the other might want to focus on athletics. Even though it's more difficult to do, it's actually better to have the child focus on both rather than having different goals from the parents. If the father wants the child to become a fierce general and the mother wants the child to become a scholar to be more of a wise king, then it will not work that well. It is better to have both the mother and father emphasizing how fierce a general should be and that he should be just as wise and have great character as the future king. They must have equal goals as a nation in order for their child to be a successful combat general and a future king as well.

The tyrant or the gentle king? – extremely strict parents vs. extremely relaxed parents

There is no right or wrong approach. But there is a reaction to every action. Self-motivation is more important than whether the player has strict or lenient parents. When the parents are too strict, players are likely to lose control when their parents aren't around to supervise them. If you don't give the players enough freedom, they will never learn to adequately guide themselves. Players that lack self-motivation but have strict parents live in a nation that could easily collapse. The players know they can't fight off the king, so they try to wait it out and let the storm pass until they get to college or become the new king. Once the player becomes the new king, the new king will not have enough competitiveness or self-motivation to reign over other kings. It's important for the player to become an independent individual who respects others before taking on the role of king.

Having a gentle king is also not ideal. Since the gentle kings don't have a fierce nature, they tend to let their generals (both the coach and the player) do whatever they want and have fun. Having fun is great in the short term, but it's not fun when you start losing. The reason many people like something or think it's fun is because they think they are good at it. If fun is the only objective, then as the win-to-loss ratio tilts toward the losses, the game becomes a lot less fun. The graceful but fierce king is ideal, which means that parents need to keep themselves balanced.

One of the good things about having two people in the role of the king is that one can be fierce and one can be comforting. Their goals can be the same, but by taking on different roles, they can help lead the nation into great battles.

The ungrateful combat general – financial pressure felt by young players

Issues related to supplies and funds affect all players, no matter their age. Young generals may not know exactly how much is being spent, but they still have some awareness based on observing the stress level and behavior of the king. The bigger the war and farther the battlefield, the more the pressure will be felt. As generals mature and grasp the importance of money, they become very cautious and start to feel immense pressure. As they battle bigger nations, if the king does not have significant resources to work with, the possibility of conquering all the nations becomes very vague and distant. It is the parents' job to stay economically stable enough for the player to stay focused on their goals. They may not be grateful of your spending, but they do feel the pressure. When players are immature, they do not know how to express their feelings of gratitude and sometimes the child takes it for granted. Regardless of who—the king or combat general—led the nation to war, it is the king's job to stay financially stable.

Interference or interests from the king – differences in coaching your own children and showing interest in their work

Kings can say whatever they want and they have the authority to do so, but the tactical general and the combat general might get annoyed if the advice is irrelevant to the military's success. Parents have the right to know how their player is training or performing. It's their job to ask questions and stay updated and in the loop. The coaches should not feel annoyed when asked to report to the parents. It's the coaches' job to report. The parents need to take the reports in a graceful way. If they are too fierce, the tactical general will be afraid to fail and stay passive. If the king is too relaxed, the tactical general will act too much on his own. Just letting the coaches know they're being supervised is enough; you don't want to micromanage them. Remember, it's up to you, until the young warrior becomes a king, to decide if the coaches are doing their job. Do not be hasty in your decisions, and be calm and wise. It's important to have the right staff at the right time. You don't need to hire the most expensive coach when you're a small nation that can't afford the best tactical general.

Your general complaining about going to battle – tantrums on and off the court in tournaments

The combat general might not be fully prepared to take on the pressure of a battle. If the combat general feels that he needed more time to prepare, then he may show it in their actions by trying to prove that he was right (which is very immature and naive). The combat general might be the one whose pride is hurt the most and who feels useless when a battle is lost, so he will be reluctant to go into battle if the preparations are not adequate for the battle at hand. It's still mostly the king's decision to go into battle and war, but the king should always discuss it with the tactical general in order for the combat general to feel comfortable in battle. The combat general might not think it's worth it to test their game, but again, when they are still in development, it's not up to the players to decide. If the situation gets worse on and off the court without any clear reason, punish the combat generals in order for them to know the seriousness of the problem, particularly if they've quit or tanked the match, but do not punish them because they lost the match. Battles are won and lost, but there is no whining on the battlefield.

They may also display a bad attitude to show the parents that they care, but that they are simply not performing well that day. It's not the correct way to show their emotions, but until someone takes action to fix the bad attitude, they won't realize what they are doing. The players need to be trained to control their emotions.

Young warriors' mindset when they go into battle – what are they thinking about when they play a match, or what do they need to think about, technique or strategy?

This is what often troubles young players. Not only is winning and losing uncertain, but the way they have to play a match is always a mystery before they go into the battlefield. The young warrior doesn't know what to focus on. It depends on what level they are at and how they are feeling that day. The better the player, the more they should think about strategy to win and not dig too deep into the small details of technique. When a shot doesn't work, they still need to think about technical adjustments to make during and in between points. Too much wanting to win can also be bad because it's hard to develop technique and a solid foundation when they are focusing only on strategy or just getting the balls back to beat the opponent. They have to figure things out on their own and learn to think independently. The key is letting the young warriors figure things out on the battlefield on their own and not interfering with their judgment on the court. All of the actions and facial expressions from the king and the tactical general can potentially affect their performance. Be strong and try to keep your emotions in check. Trying to help them in that moment may be counterproductive. Let the tactical general talk to the young warriors after the match to analyze and find solutions without being too emotional about their performance.

Taking a defeat gracefully – when your child loses in battle

It's natural for parents to feel bad when their kids lose or don't perform well. It's how they handle the situation that distinguishes good tennis parents from bad ones. When a king sends his generals to war, battles will be lost and every loss will have an impact. Discuss and analyze the situation as the king. Consider how you can help the combat general and the tactical general to be prepared for the next battle. As the king, the technical, tactical, and strategic mistakes might not be apparent. The king has the authority to advise the generals and has the right to know why the battle was lost, but the details about how to resolve the issues should be left to the tactical and combat generals. You can give them advice and express anger at the combat generals, but don't expect a high level of respect for your knowledge of war from the combat generals even when the tactical general says the same thing. Remember that respect for each level of authority is a different type of respect.

Surrendering to the enemy general – quitting or tanking a match (whining)

Players may or may not be able to explain why they surrendered to the enemy. If the player does not feel guilty for surrendering, then they are not trying hard enough in their daily lives. Something has to be done in order for the young general to understand the importance of fighting until the last breath. There's too much at stake for the king and the tactical general for the combat general to simply surrender to the enemy. It is definitely acceptable to punish the player for quitting in battle. The king does not have to explain how much is at stake and the financial resources that were spent to go into the battle. Remember that the penalty for a combat general who surrendered in ancient times was death. If a player does not even realize that they are surrendering, it is a bigger problem than purposely quitting. Make sure the player gets some type of punishment for their actions. Every time the player surrenders, the punishment should be greater than or equal to the previous punishment.

Who will be the one punishing the general? – no excuse, but the king needs to hear what they have to say

Make sure the reason for the surrender is heard before punishment is given. If there's not a very, very good reason, then punish them. Only one big punishment—preferably a tough, boring and long training exercise— should be doled out by one party, and it should be given to them right away. Do not wait until you return home or to the academy. The punishment on site will set the tone and send a message to other nations that you are not there to be defeated. Defeated generals' heads have been used to scare their enemies in the past. In the modern context, a tough punishment also sends a message to your own combat generals if you run a base camp (academy). But never sacrifice your own generals for the good of your academy. The king, drill sergeant, or the tactical general should punish the player, but not all three of them. One bold punishment is enough to make a point, but if the entire nation is criticizing the combat generals' morals, then the fighting spirit will be weakened. Kings should only punish the combat general if there is no one else that can administer punishment. Make sure the team talks it over to see who's going to punish the combat general.

Stopping or interfering with the punishment – loss of respect and unfinished punishment

When the punishment is given to the combat general, no one must interfere with the prosecution. In particular, the king should not interfere and stay silent when the combat general is being punished. If the punishment is interfered with by the king or anyone else, then the person interfering is sacrificing the respect of the person who is punishing the combat general. No matter how harsh the punishment is, they must not interfere. The person giving the punishment should consider finishing with an explanation of why it was necessary to give that harsh of a punishment to the player. If someone interferes, then the combat general may not receive the full message.

Hiring the tactician (參謀) – hiring a coach

In the next few chapters, parents will see that there are many elements a player should take into account before, during, and after the battle. This is why a coach is needed in tennis—for the experience, guidance, and management. It's nearly impossible to do all of what needs to be done with a single mind and body, especially a young one. This is also why coaching in tennis is difficult and complex. It's not just about a single aspect of technique, strategy and tactics, management, discipline, trust, ability to feel the momentum of a match, or being a role model—it's all of those things. The coaches at a higher level are paid high amounts for a reason. If your coach is priced affordably, then don't expect them to teach your child as much as a high-priced coach. Even if a capable coach is already wealthy and/or likes to help people, it is difficult for them to lower the price of their services significantly. The coach is paid mostly in respect. The prices they set represent the level of respect they deserve, and the price also serves as an indication to clients and players of how serious their services are. Remember that your tactical general has a family too. They are devoting and dedicating their lives and their family's lives to serving and helping the king and the combat general. Kings have a choice as to who they hire as a coach, but tactical generals also have a choice in who they serve. Pay respect to your tactical general and the king should have the tactical general's full loyalty.

Once the mightiest combat general or king of all the land – not all great players make great coaches

Just because they were once a great fighter doesn't mean that they turn out to be the best tactical general. Some do have awesome potential for becoming the best tactical general, but most of them can't set aside the fact that they were once a mighty king or combat general, and the act of supporting someone else is difficult due to their pride. The once-mighty king will want to play the role of the king, and the parents will waste energy trying to control them. The end result will not be a positive one. Since they do have the potential to be a great tactical general, the king must make decisions carefully and talk to them before hiring them. If they show good character and a strong heart, then it might be worth the risks of hiring them.

Hiring the famous reluctant tactical general (三顧草廬) – hiring a stubborn but famous coach

In the *Romance of the Three Kingdoms*, the king Liu Bei visited a distant land three times before hiring his strategist Zhuge Liang. Zhuge Liang knew that Liu Bei couldn't unite or conquer the lands, but Liu Bei's visit to him multiple times earned his respect and loyalty. Great coaches don't dive into a war knowing that you have a weak combat general and army. They know far too much about what must be done and how much work must be put into training the combat generals and the army. Even if the plan can be calculated, there will be obstacles and limitations to what can be done with a given army. Don't dwell on trying to understand what goes on in their brains, but give them total respect and earn their trust if you want him/her as your tactical general. While the tactical general might be very happy to see how strong the army stands physically, don't be discouraged if the tactical general is not very impressed with your combat general. The tactical general knows it's not easy diving into a war, and although it is important, they won't be too impressed by the fierceness and the outer appearance of the combat general and the troops. Figuring out how to use those troops is far more important to the tactical general.

The loyal and sincere counsel (忠臣) and the treacherous counsel (奸臣) – what the king needs to hear and what the king wants to hear

It only takes one unskilled tactical general to ruin a nation. The nation's downfall may be preventable, but the process may ruin the experience of having a coach. Once it's ruined, the king has trouble trusting the next tactical general they hire. The king must judge whether the tactical general is a loyal and sincere counsel that says what the king needs to hear or a treacherous counsel doing work for his own good and only saying what the king wants to hear. Tactical generals do make mistakes and losing one or two battles is not always their fault, but it's up to the king to decide what the best options are. They might need some more time to adjust and calculate different factors in order for them to make plans for the nation. When you decide that it's time to fire the tactical general, the king must know that just because they lost faith in this particular tactical general, that doesn't mean the next one is going to be the same. The king and the combat general still need a skilled tactical general to battle bigger nations. Asking around among different nations about a particular tactical general and their experience is an option, but you won't get the full story and it is not wise to believe everything that a different nation says. Meet up with them personally and get a feel for what they are like. Their personality, eye contact, personal story as a player, personal story as a coach, and their appearance all give hints about what kind of coach they are. Remember that a strong presence is not always the best sign. It is up to the king to judge, and the decision is not an easy one. Be wise and choose with care.

Listening to your tactical generals – guidance from your coach

When tactical generals give guidance or admonitions to the king, it's for the benefit of the nation. It is not to judge what is right or wrong or to order the king on how they should be governing, because the authority is with the king. The parents get offended sometimes when the coach tries to tell the parents what is right or wrong in raising a tennis player. The coaches are not saying that they are bad parents, nor telling the parents how to raise a child. The coaches are only giving specific instructions and information on how to help the player become a mentally strong individual for tennis. The king might think that the tactical general isn't old enough or experienced enough in raising a child to offer advice, but many coaches have gained enough experience to know and feel what's right or wrong in the realm of tennis. The kings' job is to try to understand why the tactical general might say certain things, and the job of the tactical general is to explain the reasons behind their admonitions. If the king completely blocks out the tactical generals for any reason, that's a sign of a team on the verge of breaking up.

Combat general meets tactical general – when a new coach starts coaching your player

When the tactical general is hired by the king to give advice to the combat general, they might have trust issues when training or going into the first couple of battles. A brief power struggle and pride may hinder the relationship initially. They need time to respect each other. Be aware of what is going on between the two generals. It is your job to resolve issues if the flame gets too big.

Are more tactical generals = better? – hiring multiple coaches for your player

Even if you have the best three tactical generals in the world, their mixed messages will confuse the hell out of the combat general, who must decide which type of strategy and tactics to use in combat. Every tactical general has their own beliefs and philosophy, so if there are multiple tactical generals, then the player is trying to learn different types of techniques according to which strategies and tactics the coach is trying to teach. As a young player or a young warrior, that is very confusing. Be careful of whom you hire and once you do, trust them.

The foolish king controlling the army – parents coaching tennis without solid tennis background

Imagine a parent trying to teach their child the rules of war or martial arts, but they don't have any war experience. It just isn't possible. It may work up to a certain point, but the complexities of tennis will quickly overwhelm someone that has never played competitive tennis at a high level. Even the people at the top of the game must work constantly on trying to analyze and figure out what is wrong and what is right. Whatever the goal might be for the king, hiring the right tactical general will be vital to your nation's success. If you can't afford the right tactical generals, then you're already fighting a war you can't win. Not everything goes as planned, and you'll need good advice from a tactical general to guide you through the tough times. You are the king and have absolute control, but don't try to do everything yourself.

The disrespectful, dirty, and shameless enemy combat general – handling cheaters

Whether by mistake or on purpose, bad line calls and score-changing players are present at every level. There are combat generals who use dirty tactics and any means necessary to win, but they are not respected. The generals that use dirty tactics in very obvious ways are known throughout all the nations. The pressure from the kings often causes even the most honest combat generals to use dirty tactics. When cheating happens, it's best to ask the players to handle it by calling the referee on the court. There's not much the king can do, and they should stay out of it. The king should be graceful, and if they go into the battle themselves, it does not look good. They must learn to handle the situation by staying out of the argument and asking their player to get the referee.

Score changing can't happen in pro matches that have chair umpires, but the refs do make mistakes on line calls. It actually feels significantly worse when a linesman or a chair umpire makes a mistake on a line call. If an opponent cheats, it's somewhat understandable since they want to win at all costs. When a referee makes a mistake, it's very hard to accept. It is best to think of the referees as the natural conditions and variable elements in a battle since they cannot be controlled by the king, tactical general, or the combat general.

The king going into the battlefield with the combat general – anxious parents and coaching during a match

A parent coaching during the match is like a king that doesn't know the rules of engagement diving into a battle. The child gets confused about what they need to be doing and what to focus on. The king should care but not interfere. Support them, but remember that whatever you say and do will make a difference, for better or worse, so be wise in what you say. You have authority, but they are doing the fighting. If you're emotional, then don't say anything; you've already lost your ability to think clearly.

The players get confused because you are their kings or parents. The players care about what you say, like a loyal general caring about and listening to what their king is saying. By focusing on what the parents have to say about their performance, now they have three main things to worry about: themselves, the opponent, and what their parents just said. This is why coaches are very careful with their words when players are playing a match. Besides, coaching is illegal during a match. Coaches should only speak when the advice will actually help the players. Even if the coaches know what's going on, telling the players something that won't help them will only be a distraction. Also if a tactical general asks a combat general what to do, the tactical general is speaking from experience or knows exactly what the combat general is feeling, and so they can analyze the situation much better, with less emotion, than any king that does not have combat experience.

Remember, everyone knows how much you want to say something or coach them. In the eyes of an experienced counsel, it's really a distraction. Learn to stay calm, and silence will be respected. Encourage them, but you can't fight for them.

Giving gifts, throwing parties or letting your generals relax - they are human

Everyone needs time to relax. They need fun time too. Once in a while, it's fine for them to let loose and enjoy themselves. It gives them a mental boost when you allow them to do what they enjoy, but don't let them expect that freedom on a regular basis. It's your generosity, not their privilege. Giving rewards for reaching a certain goal can also be a great tool for parents. It helps the coach and the player to be motivated, and they will get a sense that the parents are acknowledging them for their efforts.

Hiring an outside tactical general for a couple of battles - using an outside coach for a couple of tournaments.

Bringing in someone new may have short-term benefits, but most of the time, a coach hired just before a match is not able to train their players to use their tactics and strategies in the upcoming battle. It takes time to build a trusting relationship between the tactical general and the combat general. Remember that you're hiring that coach for basic preparations for the battle, not a miracle.

King to king – parents' views of other parents

Some kings are nice, and some kings aren't. You don't know when they'll be your enemy. Always be nice and show respect because they rule another nation. Being a target before the battle is never good. You can't conquer alone. You'll need friends along the way. You will need to team up to take out stronger nations. You won't know when they might be of help.

Hiring a drill sergeant (教官) – the lack of discipline, body balance, and endurance

It's easy to overlook the importance of a trainer in sports. Drill sergeants come in different forms, but I would like to think of them as the physical trainers in the tennis world. What the parents don't realize is that sometimes a trainer's job is even more important than that of the coach. Don't expect the tactical general to do the drill sergeant's work. The tactical general needs to maintain a close relationship with the combat general in order for that bond to work. The stress caused by tough fitness drills will cause a problem in their relationship. The technical stress given to the combat general by the tactical general will need their full attention and a clear mental state. It is also important for a combat general to not be reluctant about asking the tactical general a question. The drill sergeant will need the young warrior's full obedience, and it is not easy for the young warrior to switch that off when the tactical general has to do the drill sergeant's work. Although tactical generals can do some of the drill sergeants' work if the drill sergeants are not available, it is much better to hire someone with more professional experience at the job. Not only will the drill sergeant discipline and make the young warrior fit; the physical trainer will watch how the player is moving and advise the coach on what movements the player should work on improving.

Sometimes there are drill sergeants that will act like a tactical general. These coaches are often intense and work hard, but they do not focus on technical, tactical, and strategic aspects of the game. They might be inexperienced sergeants that would like to one day become a tactical general.

Wounded generals – injuries and injury prevention

Injuries happen. They are a part of the game, part of the war. Care for your general. Don't blame them for getting hurt while battling or training. You can't blame the combat general for giving their best all the time, which might cause an injury. When injuries happen outside of the battlefield, give them a warning, and let them know that they have to take care of their body better. Sometimes injuries can happen when the training is harsh, but the player is not fully alert. In this situation, the tactical general must give them warnings and explain why they have to be fully aware and alert in the training.

The great doctor (名醫) – more than rest, ice, compression, elevation

When your combat general gets injured or wounded, the king must find an adequate doctor. This task is not as easy as it sounds. Going to any doctor that specializes in the field related to the injury is one thing, but to find a great doctor, that's not an easy task. Also, doctors that specialize in sports and athletes are different from the ones you find in regular hospitals or clinics. There are also two forms of physicians: surgical doctors and physical therapists. A great option is to go to a well-known sports physical therapist. Some physical therapists approach injuries differently than surgical doctors. Often, when you visit a doctor, they'll recommend rest, ice, compression, elevation (RICE), which is good but not enough for most injuries. It takes too long for most injuries to heal with rest alone. Even if the injury does heal after a period of rest, the injured area probably still won't be ready for high-level competition, and that can lead to another injury. A sports physical therapist can get your combat general battle-ready if they know what they are doing. Again, not all sports physical therapists are equal, and you must choose them wisely.

Base camp (基地) – choosing a tennis academy

Players need a base camp where they can train and spar against other players. Look for these characteristics in a base camp: overall feel of discipline, the drill sergeant, the tactical general, and intense positive energy coming from other combat generals in training. Make sure to visit the academies you want your general to attend. Talk to the tactical generals and the drill sergeants, and watch how other players practice. Parents need to see if there's intense positive energy permeating the academy. Tennis academies may appear as if there is no order or system, but a closer look often reveals that there is more order than you originally noticed. Some focus on technique, some focus on discipline, and some focus on tactics and strategy. It's difficult to find the perfect academy, so try to analyze what your young general needs and pick the right academy for your general.

Training camps (训练所) – sending kids to academies by themselves

Sending your young generals to a training camp has advantages and disadvantages. The young general will learn to be independent, but that takes time and many kids are not ready to be independent. If the academy does not teach the young warriors good habits and lifestyles, then no matter how great the academy is for tennis, it will be difficult to control your generals when they come back from training camp.

Good habits and lifestyles – learned from the parents' lifestyles

A healthy lifestyle and good habits must be learned with the help of positive role models and guidance. If the tactical general and drill sergeant are not spending enough time with the young warrior, the king must step in and assist as they are the parents of the warrior. Here are just a few of the things that will help your young general: eating right, stretching, shadow motion, taking care of yourself, not getting injured off the court, jackets in cold buildings, sleeping habits, staying fit, doing rehab, and warming up properly. Good habits will prepare them for the unexpected and allow them to be ready for the opportunity that might be just around the corner. Efforts must be made beforehand to help them be physically and mentally ready for any type of battle.

Successor of the throne (承繼)

Once the young warrior matures and conquers a lot of the big nations, it's time to pass on the throne to the combat general. The timing of passing on the throne is crucial to the young warrior. Too early and they go out of line, too late and you'll be holding them back. Usually this process happens naturally with the young warrior conquering some of the big nations that people didn't expect. Regardless, there will be a time when the king has to let go and let the heir take full responsibility for their actions. Prepare them wisely and fiercely, and they will be ready.

If this seems like a lot of work, that's because it is. And that makes the parents feel like they should have a say in everything, but the kings must be careful with their words, as the words of the king are the most powerful weapon.

II.

COACHES – TACTICAL GENERAL (参謀), THE BRAINS, AND OVERALL GUIDANCE

The tactical general's role is to advise the king and help the combat generals to be victorious in battles. Many people don't understand the importance of coaching in the lower levels, particularly those that are new to competitive tennis. While combat generals might have the ability to do the fighting in a battle, they might not have a good grasp of the big picture in a battle and the war as a whole. The coach is able to see the big picture from the sidelines and as a third party. They can also zoom in on details to help the player form solid foundations.

This section will not be covering the obvious aspects of coaching. This section will be about the troubles and challenges coaches might face while trying to maintain a good relationship with the king and the combat general. It will help the king and the combat generals understand the role of a coach and help tactical generals earn respect from the king and the combat generals.

Role of a tactical general – leader and supporter

Everyone wants to be a leader nowadays. Tactical generals need to be great leaders, but they also have to know their role of supporting the king. The tactical generals play a vital role in helping the king to conquer all the nations and helping the combat general to fight efficiently and effectively in battles. Some tactical generals like to act as if they are the king in the tennis world, but by comparing a tactical general of a nation to a coach, you can see that they are not the king. Tactical generals may ask for and spend a nation's funds, but they are not responsible for bringing in the funds, nor do they fight the battles for the combat general. So what's so special about the coach?

The experiences as a warrior and a king (?!) – trying to understand the coach

It might be difficult for the king and the young warrior to fully understand, but the coach has been to many battlefields, has endured some of the toughest training camps, and they know how to prepare for battles. They have fought and survived great battles, they've made mistakes and paid the consequences, and they also might have been a king before. Most of the experiences that the young warrior is facing and the troubles that the king is going through have already been experienced first-hand by these tactical generals. They've survived in the toughest times, yet the glorious days have not yet come for these tactical generals. They might even be called failures, yet they are still ready. Ready to take on the world again.

The parents and the players think they are going through one of the toughest times in their lives and wonder if anyone else has felt like this before. They often completely overlook the troubles that a coach went through as a player once, including countless hours of practice, all the tears and sweat, all the sacrifices, watching and feeling the troubles of their parents and siblings, watching the family break up into pieces, watching their fellow players struggle. There are many untold stories, but no one wants to hear them. The kings (parents) expect their stories to be different. The young warrior is far too immature to understand.

The supporting act - it's not about you (coach), don't expect them to understand

The coach must not expect the king and the young warrior to understand the troubles that they have been through. They are not very interested in the stories of a person that has failed to become the ruler of all nations. The tactical generals' job is to help the king and the young warrior to become the biggest nation that they can be. Notice the words "that they can be"; for the tactical generals, there are no happy endings. They will not realize their own limitations as the king or the combat general and will instead blame the tactical general. When the king has succeeded in conquering some nations, the glory goes to the king and the combat general, not the tactical general.

Talking to the king, tactical general's superior – with class and dignity yet compassionate

When consulting or meeting with the king for the first time, the tactical general does not have to be so fierce and upfront. Stay on point with what you have to say and answer the king's questions using words that they can understand and relate to. When using technical and advanced words, the king will get confused. If you are elaborate, flashy, and overconfident with your words, a naive king will think that you are the best tactical general in the world. But once the naive king realizes that you are not victorious right away, then you will get executed. Answer questions and get a feel for how much respect they have for you.

Price of lessons and services (給料) – price vs. respect

When a king respects your importance, worth, and your belief in the nation, a price can be negotiated. The gap between what you should get paid and what you're actually getting paid will be filled with respect. A king who doesn't know the importance of a coach should not get any discounts, even if you believe in the combat general. Tactical generals should price their services low enough so they can provide services beyond their set price. Again, any gap will be filled with respect.

The ultimate test of the king and the tactical general (諫言) – admonition/remonstration

The biggest challenge for a tactical general is clearly explaining the current situation to the king. It is difficult to explain to the king with total respect and honesty why they lost a battle or why they won, particularly if the king does not have a full understanding of the game of tennis. The coaches and players, tactical generals and the combat generals, usually have mutual respect. Even if they argue about an issue, they can usually reach an agreement because they have a better understanding of tennis than the parents. If the parents have played tennis professionally, then that's like having a king who has been a war general before, and there are pros and cons to parents having more knowledge about tennis.

An honest coach can be very difficult for parents to listen to. The parents have to stay calm and clear-minded, and view things as a third party. It can be nerve-racking and possibly cost the coach his job if he tells parents the blunt truth. In the stories of the warring nations, even the most loyal strategists and cabinet members who told the tyrant the unvarnished truth often received the death penalty. The coach has to be clear and to the point when making suggestions or informing the parents and be prepared to answer questions and explain the proposed resolutions to the problems. The tactical general must be able to tell the king the truth, but in an easily understandable way. Again, being elaborate and telling them all the details won't do the coach any good. You also don't want to tell them too little. It's a balancing act, and if you don't have their full respect, you must be able to read their reactions and stay psychologically on top of the king. Do not be afraid of losing your job; if the king is wise, he will listen. At the same time, be wise with your words and balance is key.

Sacrificing themselves as a tactical general or an advisor – the coaches should have a life too

Some loyal coaches feel that they must devote their entire life to serving the king and the combat generals. There are sacrifices that must be made, but the job shouldn't consume their entire life. Throughout history, advisors who have gone to great lengths to influence the king's decision making, sadly, have almost never convinced the king to change his mind. Great patience is required when trying to convince the parents or the players to make one decision or another. Often, time is the only resolution to their stubbornness.

If the tactical general is married, he should listen to what his wife has to say. She may be the only one he can fully trust. She can keep the tactical general grounded and offer new perspectives (reality check). Sometimes the tactical generals have been living a mission-focused lifestyle for so long, they have a hard time living a balanced life. The wife might have difficulties understanding the tactical general and why anyone would be happy living like that. For the tactical general, it feels like a duty; you do this because it makes you satisfied and happy. Your wife can help you live a more well-rounded life. Take care of your loving wife (spouse).

Tactical general asking for total control – ignoring the roles of parents

The tactical generals must not avoid talking to the king. This will only cause bigger problems in the end. If it is tough to advise the king, then the tactical general should step down gracefully or ask to take a break. If the tactical general assumes full responsibility for a nation, the king and the combat general might have trouble determining who should have the various roles. If the king gives the tactical general total control but then starts to interfere with his decision making, the team's sense of unity may start to break down.

Keeping the king happy – relationship between the coach and the player

A common mistake that many tactical generals make is viewing the young warrior as the king. The tactical general knows sacrifices have to be made and that total loyalty is essential, but trying to serve the immature heir to the throne is very naive of a tactical general. It is very important for the tactical general to maintain good relationships with the combat generals/young warriors, but they are not yet kings. They need to be taught and be disciplined. The young warrior will act like a king and wants to be a king, but he/she is not the king yet.

Training the army without the supervision of the king – working

hard to improve the player when the parents are not present on the court

If the coach slacks off when the parents are not there, the consequences are much more serious than they would be if the parents were present because the blame goes to the coach, not the player, when they are not performing. The coach needs to be able to push the player even if the parents are not able to come out to the courts. There are different aspects of the player's game a coach can work on with or without the parents on the court. The coach must use their time wisely to improve different aspects of the player's game when the parents are not present on the court.

Gifts, rewards, and vacations from the king - not a privilege, do not expect them

When the tactical general receives unexpected gifts and rewards from the king, it should be viewed simply as a sign of the generosity and considerate nature of the king. The tactical general should not view the gifts as a bonus for their coaching, which can lead to arrogance.

Talking to your combat general – similar to talking to your young self when you were the young warrior

Be ready to answer questions when you're talking to your combat general. They need to question your tactics and strategies in order for them to fully believe in them during the battle or the war. The tactical general should try to remember all the troubles they went through and what it was like to be a young warrior. The times might be different and the tactical general must be careful not to sound like they are bragging about the past. They must try to relate to the young warrior as best they can without dwelling on how great they were in the past. Stories are great, but the tactical general must make sure the story is told based on what it is that they are trying to explain. Keep the stories short, on point, and interesting, and what is not questioned doesn't need to be answered. Not all combat generals have a mind that can handle all of your creative tactical ideas.

In the middle of the king and the combat general – the middle man: serious and polite to the king and a source of enjoyment for the combat generals

The goals of the king are clear; the king wants to reign over other nations. The goals of combat generals are not as clear sometimes. The combat generals just try to survive each day and enjoy the battles themselves. For the combat generals, war is just a game. The coach's job is to be the middle man. Be clear and concise on what needs to be done and report to the king and prepare the generals so the generals can enjoy the battles. Most of the time, the goal for the generals is to have fun dominating others. They are less interested in all the glory and fame, but they do enjoy making their enemies suffer. Keeping this in mind, the coach needs to find ways to help the combat generals enjoy the battles even more. There are numerous ways to help the combat generals love the battles. Some of the ways that coaches can help combat generals include: enforcing and teaching solid fundamentals to add power, consistency, and accuracy; helping them understand the game; teaching them strategies and tactics so cunning that they may feel like they are cheating. All of these methods can be used to make the combat generals feel that they can dominate other combat generals. As these methods are taught and enforced, it does not always have to be in a serious and strict way. Unless they need discipline, the methods can be taught in a fun way with plenty of laughter and enjoyment.

Training and disciplining the young warrior – discipline vs. abuse

The players at the top level of national and international juniors and the touring pros do not get to that stage without any discipline. There is a fine line between abuse and discipline, but what distinguishes the two is the mindset of the player and the coach and not how other people view them. If the coach is scolding the player, but he does so with purpose and a good heart, it is discipline. If the coach is scolding the player based on their personal feelings or purpose, then it is abuse. Disciplining the player and pushing them to the limit mentally and physically is a part of the job of guiding the junior player in the right direction. Many coaches and parents don't know the difference between the two. Even if the parents know the difference, they are not very good at suppressing their personal feelings/emotions and really disciplining the player for the player's sake.

It is important for the player to have the right mindset to be able to take the tough discipline. The issue often is not whether the coach can discipline the player. It's difficult to find players that are able to take the discipline the right way. At the top level, the game is extremely competitive. Competing at that level requires total focus, which means the players will not enjoy their training all the time. Since the majority of the fun and enjoyment comes from winning, players need to appreciate and believe in discipline. Most players that are at the top level in any age division or at the pro level are there because they were able to endure the discipline and the training that they received. Although physical beating should not be condoned at any time by a coach, most types of punishment and disciplinary action can be justified if the coach has the player's long-term interests at heart. Sometimes, even if the coach has a good heart, it is ultimately up to the player to determine later in life whether the punishment and discipline received were correct (with good heart) or incorrect (abuse). Such a judgment may depend on how healthy the player's mind is, and not necessarily on the results of their tennis career.

Regulating the young warrior – compassionate vs. merciless

The tactical general needs to be able to regulate the combat general. At different times, the coach may need to be compassionate or merciless, depending on the situation. The coach needs to be able to sense what is best for the situation. If a player is at their mental breaking point or mentally exhausted from battling constantly, they might need a break, and being compassionate can actually boost the player's energy and help them be prepared to go back to the battlefield after a short break.

Not only is timing important, but it also may depend on how mature the player is. If the player is not ready to play at a highly competitive level, then it is best to not use merciless ways to handle the player. Another difficult situation may arise if the parents are tough on the players without any clear reasons or goals. If the parents are not good role models, and are trying to discipline the players without understanding them, the player will feel lost. The coach's toughness is grounded in experience, because they have been through something similar themselves and know that mental toughness is a huge part of the game. The players can usually take the mercilessness from the coach because the players know unconsciously that the coach probably went through the same thing when they were a player. The coach must be truly compassionate to the players and try to understand them first. Once the player is mature and has enough belief and trust, the coach can be merciless to the player to prepare them for the battles that they will have to endure. Getting to know how each player feels and thinks is very important to be able to give them the right preparation.

Maturing combat general – staying knowledgeable and respected

Tactical generals need to keep studying the art of war to be able to make the right calculations and offer up-to-date advice on training and tactics. The young general will need to improve different parts of their game at different points in their lives. To stay relevant and respected, the tactical general must stay abreast of the game's latest tactics, strategies, equipment, techniques, and other elements. The tactical general should be able to teach and help build their foundations without imposing strategies, tactics, or techniques based on their own experiences. As the young generals mature, they will start to have thoughts of their own. If the tactical general is too pushy with their tactics, the players will not have any room for their own growth and creativity. Also, the level of your students does not define you as a coach. Keep trying to get better and improve yourself, and when the opportunity arises to coach someone great, you will be ready.

The perfect tactical general – over-confident coach

There's nothing more dangerous than an over-confident coach who doesn't know much and only speaks and doesn't listen, or who tries to change a player based on a style he likes. Try to listen to the combat general and hear them out when they have trouble or when they offer input on battle tactics. The tactical general must think about why the combat general would say the things they say. If you can't understand, then sometimes it's better to let the players figure things out on their own and let them try to explain to you why it makes sense. The players will respect the coach even more when they applaud their creativity (as long as it's not something ridiculous) or admit that they don't know the answer to a question rather than giving the players an off-the-cuff answer. If the tactical general does not have a solution for the problem, then they can research it to get ready to answer that question in the future.

Giving some space to the combat general - they need time to learn about themselves

Combat generals need time to learn about themselves, and the information that you've given them might take some time to employ in the real battlefield. Let them have some time for themselves and go out into the battlefield alone to test their knowledge and skills. Playing practice sets with the tactical general watching is great, but it's not an accurate gauge of performance since the wins and losses don't matter as much. When they need this time, do not be afraid of losing your brave general. When they are ready, they'll come back. The two generals should talk about what has worked and hasn't worked. After taking the data from the combat general, the tactical general should train them accordingly.

Zooming in and out of the battlefield – ability to see the technical, tactical, mental, and the overall flow of the game

The tactical general should be able to read and see the battle in detail, at the troop level and the big picture, which is the flow of the battle. The coach should be able to spot the small technical errors, but also be able to understand and feel the flow of the entire match. The tactical general must know what is affecting the player's ability to play effectively. Often, a player has the right strategy, but he/she can't implement it because they do not know how to hit a shot correctly. Once the tactical general figures out why a player plays a certain way by listening to them and understanding them, the players can be changed quite easily. Tweaking technique can be a daunting task for both generals, and it takes a significant amount of effort and time, but it's imperative to add new shots and variety into the combat general's overall game plan and change a player at a fundamental level. Watch for technical (technique, body balance, and footwork), endurance, mental, overall composure, tactical, and strategical errors.

Leadership before going into war – leadership before going to tournaments

Everything may go smoothly while in training, but players often get sensitive and irritable before tournaments. This is normal because of the pressure they feel before going into battle—especially if they haven't played a tournament or a big event for a while. Every feeling will be amplified, making it seem like a big deal. Just like a soldier being scared and anxious before going into war, players will feel nervous, and the uncertainty may start to overwhelm them. Make sure you lead them with discipline and use whatever methods necessary to help the player get over the feelings of anxiety. Giving in to anxiety can lead to under-training before a tournament. The player might give up on one day of training, in hopes of feeling better the next day. That is usually not the case, and whatever the player is uncertain about has to be discussed, and the coach and the player must come up with a solution before the tournament.

Picking battles – choosing which pro and high-level junior tournaments to play

Picking which tournaments to play is more art than science. This is more important for a player that is starting to play at the pro level and Junior ITFs and not so much at the national junior tournaments. It's difficult to predict which tournament may be weak this year. The coach must be experienced enough to know the general flow of the movement in the nations in the current year, and use data from the previous year to be able to make assumptions. Usually the kings decide where they would like to take the battle, but with data and good reasoning from the tactical general, the kings can be persuaded.

Picking easy battles to fight is not cowardly. It's wise to grow your nation (accumulate points) by conquering small and defenseless nations in order to be able to battle bigger nations. Winning is never certain and calculating wise use of the resources is absolutely necessary.

Constantly checking the health of your generals – injury prevention and rehab training

It is critical for a tactical general to frequently check the health of their combat generals. Injuries can not only affect the performance of the combat generals, but they can be very costly for the king. When changing equipment or technique, the tactical generals must do everything possible to prevent pain or further injury. Good rehab and injury prevention habits can be taught by the tactical general and the drill sergeant to prolong the combat general's career. The responsibility for implementing the training lies with the drill sergeant and the combat general. If there is no drill sergeant, the tactical general has some responsibility, but it is mostly the combat generals' responsibility to keep their body in good shape.

Disciplining your combat generals – teaching them correct and proper routines and having respect for others

Discipline is not about yelling at your generals for no reason. Discipline should be focused on teaching them correct and proper routines and how to respect others. There must be rules and if the rules are broken, there should be sufficient punishment. If the tactical general is too lenient, the player will fall out of line and become rude, impolite, and ill-mannered. For inexperienced players, the rules and punishments can be a little more lenient until they are ready to play competitively.

Recruiting or taking combat generals from other nations – taking players from other academies or coaches

A history of taking combat generals from other nations will make the other tactical generals very wary of you. Unless a king approaches you, you should not approach the generals first. Be a likeable and respectable tactical general and the combat generals and the kings will notice. Maintain your class and dignity. There are other ways to recruit players; don't consider taking someone unless you believe in them wholeheartedly. Even after you take a combat general from other nations, try to maintain a good relationship with other tactical generals and give them respect.

Base camp crumpled – fall of an academy

There are several ways a base camp could fail. If an academy is too big, the tactical general may not able to effectively hire and manage lower-ranked generals or drill sergeants. Other serious problems may include: failure to keep the kings happy, setting up an academy in an area unfit for competitive tennis, undisciplined combat generals, not enough funds or other resources. There are different factors that need to be considered. Just because you are a great tactical general, that doesn't mean you can run a base camp. Do your calculations and proceed with care.

Blank ammunition training – hitting with dead balls

Coaches that teach with dead balls are like generals training with blank rounds/ammunition for training. The coach should have the right type of balls for more realistic training and for the players to get used to the balls used in tournaments. Parents and unsuspecting combat generals don't usually care, but when you go to a tournament and have to readjust to a different type of ball, that's another variable that the combat general has to take into account. If the same balls can't be used, similar balls should be used before going to tournaments.

Combat general to the new king – junior to pro, the difference between pro and amateur/juniors

Many thought processes have to change when the player arrives at the pro level. Eventually, tennis is a game for the combat generals and they have to learn to enjoy it. The player has to get creative and learn to use the knowledge and experience they have acquired during their combat general years. Respect may be one-sided when players are young, but as they gain knowledge and experience, it's more important for the coach to start respecting the players' thoughts and actions. Coaches must help players reach that state by guiding them to think on their own, but within the boundaries of right and wrong. The pro player has to enjoy battling it out with the opponent and enjoy trying to dominate the opponent. The fun in tennis is in dominating your opponent with your style of play and strategy, not just hitting the ball over the net and into the lines.

Manipulation and anticipation – reading minds and actions from experience and calculations to act and react to the situations

The coaches' most powerful weapon is their ability to calculate based on their experience and knowledge. The coach has more knowledge and experience than the parents and the players. Because of all their experience and knowledge, tactical generals can manipulate and anticipate the actions of others. The ability to see what others can't, manipulation, and anticipation are the best weapons a coach has—so they must speak and act wisely to guide them to victory

III.

PLAYERS – COMBAT GENERAL (將軍) AND THE PLATOONS (小隊)

Have you ever wondered why it's so hard being a tennis player? By comparing the players to combat generals, players will have a better understanding of why it's so tough. In this chapter, the player is compared to a combat general in relation to warfare. The player has very similar roles to the combat generals and the platoons. The comparison to a combat general can explain why most players are so focused on their routines and so superstitious. The combat generals control the platoons and the army in the battlefield, and improvise tactics and strategies in order to defeat the enemy. Outside of the battlefield, the relationships with parents and coaches are similar to those of the king and the tactical general.

This section was written in hopes of helping the players fight on the court like a fierce general by giving them a clear understanding of how they should mentally and physically prepare for battle; how they should fight on the battlefield without quitting; and develop a better understanding of the king (parents) and the tactical general (coach). Some of the context might be difficult to understand when the players are young, but as they mature, they should be able to better understand these guidelines.

The role of the combat general – love for tennis and the competition

The combat generals might not believe in all of the philosophies the king espouses, but they are loyal and they trust in their king unconditionally. The combat generals love to battle, and whatever their weapon of destruction may be, they love to dominate others and are relentless in their offensive and defensive tactics. Even though the odds are often against them, they always fight hard with an endless passion to win. In the end, war is just a game for the combat generals.

The player needs to love tennis in order for them to withstand the long years of rigorous training and all the battles on the road as a warrior, and to fight off other nations when they become kings themselves. The combat generals should love to compete and fight for themselves.

The strong connection but inconsiderate king – player-to-parent relationship

The strong connection between the king and the combat general can't be ignored. Both want to dominate the other nations. The king needs the combat general to do the fighting and the combat general needs the king's support for them to continue their game of war. They both need each other, but they rarely have a good understanding of each other.

Usually, the king does not have any idea how it feels to go out on the battlefield alone. They might try to understand using other related subjects, but they will not have a full understanding of what the combat general is going through out on the battlefield. Just because the parents play tennis recreationally doesn't mean they have a full understanding of what it feels like to be a real general. Recreational tennis and competitive tennis are totally different ball games. Still, the job of the king is not an easy job. Combat generals have no idea how much work the king has; it's hard to even imagine. The combat general should respect the king for who they are and the belief in the players.

Talking to the king – your coach is your best bet to be a bridge of understanding

When the king asks combat generals questions, sometimes it's difficult for the combat generals to explain to the king what they are doing out on the battlefield. Just because the king does not have a clear understanding of what goes on in the battlefield, it does not mean that the combat general and the tactical general should be ignoring the king. The king has the right to know what has happened. It is best to talk with the tactical general to analyze together what happened on the battlefield and find an easy way to explain it to the king. Even though it hurts the most for the combat generals when the battle is lost, the king takes the losses personally as they feel like they've lost the battle. Try not to feed the flame by confronting the king directly when they are still enraged about a lost battle.

Preparing for training and battle – not just a mindset, checking equipment and preparing supplies

Training and battle prep begins way before the combat generals go into training or go out into the battlefield. Gripping rackets, taking extra grips, extra shirts, towels, shoes, rackets, checking string conditions, hats, water, and other equipment checks and prep should be done by the player. It is the combat general's job to check his/her weapons and equipment before going to training or to battle. Do not expect someone else to do the job for you. If someone else is doing that job and leaves out an important piece of equipment, it is the combat generals' fault for not checking all the equipment before going to battle or training. They must learn to prepare their equipment themselves for battles and training.

The players might not be able to drive, do the laundry, or buy equipment themselves, but it is their job to let their parents know that they need something. It is foolish for anyone to think that these jobs can be done by the young generals alone. Eventually, the players will have to do everything by themselves, and it's better to learn to get prepared as early as you can.

Outer appearance – the way people view you as a player

There are many ways players can present themselves: humble, cocky, confident, shy, quiet, loud, nice, rude, ignorant, caring, etc. It is best to lie low and stay under the radar when going into a tournament. Inner confidence has nothing to do with lying low or staying under the radar. Once you're not a threat, you won't be a target. Until you gain enough power, stay low. It may seem like a cowardly move, but it will help your long-term survival. Don't let people know that you're smart. There's nothing more stupid than letting everyone know that you're smart. That also applies to talking about your abilities before a tournament. You don't go into enemy territory before the war with war drums playing as loud as you can—unless that's a strategy to scare the small nations. Be confident, but stay low.

All the traits related to being a fierce warrior don't make you a likeable character. You don't have to make it even worse by showing off to everyone that you are not their friend. Work on your soft side, appearance-wise. If you appear to be too strong, then they can see your intentions too well. Outside of the battlefield, being friendly, humble, accepting faults, and appearing slightly gullible all have the same effects. It's smoke to hide your true self. Try to hide your true self, but do not lose yourself. It's easy to get confused since you may not yet know your true self. Whatever the outer appearance might be, one's true self should always be full of ambition and killer instincts.

The eyes of the tiger and killer instincts – confidence and training

Confidence comes from the right practice and training. Discipline is a part of the correct training, but it also has another purpose. You train hard to form a habit. You train hard to become unpredictable. You train hard to expect the unexpected. The tougher the training, the more you find out you hate to lose. Remember that for the combat general, battling is just a game, and losing is not fun. The sacrifices and hard work will ultimately help you enjoy the game. Learn to enjoy the tough training.

Anyone who says you should just have fun in practice is not really helping you to reach a competitive level. You need to find someone that can help you win and hit better shots so you can enjoy hitting as well.

Expecting the unexpected: do as your drill sergeant tells you – fitness, rehab, and endurance training

The importance of good habits and regular fitness training cannot be emphasized enough. Fitness and endurance training is not just for winning a match; it's to prepare for the worst. Listen to your drill sergeant and do what he says. The drill sergeant will prepare you for the upcoming battles; do not complain. If you can't withstand the tough but systematic training that the drill sergeants make you do, then you won't make it because you're not training enough. If you don't make it through the workouts because you are afraid that you'll get hurt, then you won't make it because you are too weak. Either way, you won't be able to survive all the battles. Battles can be won, but you won't win the war without proper training from the drill sergeants.

Don't blame the drill sergeant for your failures, when they are trying to prepare you for war and you get hurt. You might be the one that's too weak or weak-minded. It is not up to the player to decide if the training is too tough. That decision is made by the king and the tactical general. You do not question the drill sergeant. You do. You'll thank them later.

Training to the max and pushing beyond the limits – second wind

Why do players need to be pushed to the limit? Players need to feel the effects of the second wind, the phenomenon that happens when the body is pushed to the limit and the player feels a sudden surge of energy to press on at top performance level with less exertion. If a player has never felt the phenomenon of second wind, they have not pushed themselves to the limit yet. The players often can't push to the limit alone since the mind and body want to be comfortable. Once the wall has been hit, it's normal to want to stop. The stage at which the second wind happens far exceeds a state of being tired. Before you feel a second wind, every muscle in your body will burn, you will see colors differently, and be almost unable to move because of pain in every inch of your body. When the second wind hits, the breath that you take will seem cool and fresh even on the hottest day, the body feels pain, but it becomes manageable, and the mind will be clear of all negativity. Systematic training is all good, but in order to feel the second wind, excruciating training has to be done. If the player hasn't felt the phenomenon of second wind, then they do not deserve to beat other players that have. The player probably won't be able to defeat the ones who have because they do not have the same mental toughness and physical tolerance as the ones who feel second wind constantly in training. The players that have received this type of training hate to lose, not only because they've spent their time in training, but they cannot accept losing because of how hard they have trained.

Battling with fatigue and minor wounds – playing with soreness during training and in matches.

Try to enjoy being sore during training. The training that the player has done the prior day will affect how they move and think on the court. Training to play with soreness will help you be prepared for tournaments. When sore in training, suck it up and continue. The time will come when you have to play sore the next match. The enemy generals will be relentless. You'll have to play sore and with wounds from the earlier battles. If you're lucky, you'll get a pushover general, but you won't always be that fortunate. Even if they are a pushover, you will still have to fight to beat them. Don't take them lightly.

How much time players take in between points depends on how they feel. Feel sluggish? Speed things up in between points, jump around, and walk faster to wake up. Feeling very tired but you can feel yourself recovering or feeling rushed? Slow it down and take your time in between points. There is no rule for how you should use that time. Use it wisely, depending on how you feel that day.

Controlling emotions – expectations and expecting the worst

Just because the training went well yesterday, there's no guarantee that you will play well in the match today. Just because you played badly yesterday, there's no guarantee that you will play badly and lose today. Just because you won the battle today, there is no guarantee that you will win tomorrow. Don't get too emotional over losses and wins. More battles are imminent and the emotions will get in the way. No battles are the same and no enemies are the same.

Expecting to play as well as the day before is dangerous. Although the player can be confident, there are too many variables and conditions that change from day to day, to expect too much from the player. Keep your emotions in check and try to clear your mind in order to make accurate judgments about the situation and analyze your opponents precisely.

Communication with the tactical general – bidirectional communication

There should be mutual respect between the tactical general and combat general. It's acceptable to question the tactical general. It's fine to question the goals and the meaning of their teachings or strategies. The combat general has to fully understand what it is they are doing on the battlefield in order to believe in the overall plan. If the tactical general is unclear of the directions or the intentions are not understood by the combat general, the combat general will be confused while on the battlefield. It is up to the combat general to follow the guidance of a tactical general or to change and improvise to handle the current situation.

Players often think that the way to show respect to the tactical general is to listen to them in silence. Just listening to what the tactical general is saying and not saying a word or asking questions is not giving them respect. If the player does not understand, they should be asking questions to gain a clear understanding of what needs to be done. Ask the tactical generals in a respectful way and try to question them in regard to what the conversation at hand is about. The questions are not to test the tactical generals; they are intended to prevent any confusion and come to an agreement.

The mightiest and fiercest general of all the land, Lu Bu – players that don't listen and only believe in themselves

Lu Bu (呂布) was a military general and warlord who lived in the late Eastern Han dynasty. His martial arts capabilities were hailed as the best under the skies (馬中赤兔 人中呂布). Trusting only his abilities and talents, he switched allegiances erratically and freely betrayed his allies and was noted for his poor planning and management skills. He couldn't obey the orders of anyone but himself. He trusted only himself and jumped around from nation to nation. He was always suspicious of others and unable to control his subordinates. All of these factors ultimately led to his downfall.

The war can't be fought alone. It's good to stay confident as a player, but you'll need to trust in your allies and listen to your tactical generals to fight at your maximum potential. Become a respectable general and learn to listen, think, and act wisely. Brute force and natural talent are not always the keys to success.

Inevitable and under-prepared battles – not wanting to play tournaments and matches

The king and the tactical general might make you go into the battlefield even if you do not want to or might not be fully prepared for battle.

Whatever the reason is, do what you can to survive. It won't be fun, but it's inevitable. Discussing it with your king and the tactical general might be a solution, but without any promising history of proper preparation and hard training from the combat general, the king will criticize you.

Into the battlefield with a knife instead of a gun – going into a match without confidence

Warriors don't complain; they fight and survive with what they have. If you are not confident going into a match, remember your opponent could be feeling even worse. If your everyday weapon is a cannon, but it's broken, you might have to go into the battlefield with only a handgun. You might only have a handgun going into a battle and be scared, but they might be coming to the battle with a knife. Try to fight the best you can with what you have for that day. Stay strong and do not let your enemies know of your weakness.

Nervousness before battles – sensitivity and feeling the pressure before matches and tournaments

There's not one general or tennis player that does not feel any nervousness before a match or a tournament. As the next tournament approaches, you will feel very aggravated at all the small things that may make you under-perform in a match. Any bad feelings that you have will be amplified, and they will suddenly feel like a huge deal. Being super-sensitive before matches or tournaments is normal for players. Discipline must be enforced to be able to handle the pressure. Once you can't cope with the pressure, you will resort to tanking or whining. You won't be able to fight at your highest level until you are able to use the pressure and sensitivity to your advantage. Heightened sensitivity is what can give you the ability to feel the changes in the environment for you to adapt to the circumstances. Discipline is needed to be able to cope with the stress of the heightened senses and pressure, and channel the energy to use it against the opponent, not yourself.

The level of your tennis in practice and in matches is usually different. The level of your tennis at practice and training is the potential level you can reach once you familiarize yourself with the uncertainty of playing a match or tournaments. The level of your tennis with pressure added in matches and a couple of days before the tournament is your true level. In order for you to play well in matches, you need to constantly be pressured by playing tournaments as often as you can, and discipline yourself in training by constantly dealing with pressure. Nervousness comes from uncertainty. By experiencing uncertainty, uncertainty becomes familiar. Being familiar with uncertainty creates the ability to handle the nerves. Get familiar with uncertainty and expect the unexpected. No matter how confident you are in practice or how much you have perfected your game in practice, the feeling of uncertainty never changes before playing a match or in tournaments. The only way to cope with it is to experience it over and over to learn how to handle the sensitivity and use it as positive energy. As you learn how to handle different types of situations, the feeling of uncertainty will become less, but it will never go away. It never should go away completely because it helps you sense the changes in your opponents and environment and get ready to adapt to different circumstances.

Into the battlefield – decisions in the match

Once the battle starts, all of the decision making is up to the combat general. There is no one to help them. They must rely on their training and the tactics and strategies given by the tactical general to defeat the enemy. Remember that all the decisions in the match are up to the combat general. The king does not have a clear understanding of how a battle should be fought. When the battle is over and the king asks why you've decided to take certain actions, it might be because the king has difficulty understanding what the combat general was trying to do. Since the actions of the young combat generals are instinctive and reactive rather than proactive, the combat generals cannot analyze why they've taken such actions most of the time. As young generals, it is tough for them to control and calculate all of the platoons and the variables that are happening inside the battlefield. As the combat general matures, they should be able to analyze and calculate the situation better to stay proactive in battle.

Staying focused in battle – concentration and self-talk

Out on the court, it is easy to get distracted by other courts, outside environments, and thinking too many things at once. Although tennis players' minds need to be flexible, focusing on one thing at a time can help you stay focused in the match. The mind has a habit of thinking about many things at once without organizing the thoughts. Try to say things out loud to yourself to focus on one thing at a time. Although the mind can think of lots of things at once, you can only say one thing at a time with your mouth. Once you're used to talking to yourself out loud, then start talking to yourself internally to keep your thoughts organized. Even during the point, when a specific situation happens, you can scream at yourself internally to stay alert. If speaking to yourself out loud works the best, keep talking to yourself out loud in between points. Don't worry about how others will think of you while you talk to yourself. People will not think you're crazy; they'll think that you're focused.

Improvising on the battlefield – pre-calculations are not always correct

There are moments in a battle where the combat general has to improvise tactics that were not provided by the tactical general. This decision in battle might have a huge impact on winning or losing. The combat general should be ready to improvise during a battle. Nothing goes precisely according to plan no matter how much pre-calculation is done with the tactical general.

Do not come out of a match regretting that you only followed the directions of your king or your tactical general. Try your own tactics against the enemy. It might be the best decision in the battle. Trust your instincts and believe in yourself. Try different tactics within the limits of your abilities and tools that you have trained with, and the king and the tactical general will praise you for trying different tactics. Remember that they are not always right and it's up to you to judge out on the battlefield. Try to strike a balance between using the techniques and skills learned in practice and improvising.

Signs from the tactical general – signs from the coach or parents during a match

During the battle, the tactical general might give signals to help the combat generals. If you are not sure of what the tactical general is signaling, then it's best to ignore it completely. It's tough to think about the task at hand and try to figure out what the tactical general is asking the combat general to do. This situation rarely happens if the tactical general is experienced, and it is against the rules for anyone to be coaching during the match. It's good to get mental support from the tactical general during the match by looking at them once in a while, but any signals from outside can get confusing if the signs aren't clear. The combat general should try to keep his/her head in the match and not focus on what's happening outside of the battlefield.

Losing weapons in battle – losing the feel of a shot during a match

It happens—your backhand doesn't work all of a sudden. Or serve or forehand. Whatever it is, don't quit. You survive. There's too much at stake. Quitting tells the people around you that you don't care. Don't break that chain. Quitting or surrendering is much more devastating than losing. Can't win? Lose hard. Find a different way. Show the enemy that you won't go down easily. Training can be done to get better and fix problems, and the strategy can be rethought in the next match. Quitting is not acceptable.

The ultimate sin, surrendering to the enemy general – quitting or tanking a match

There's no excuse for quitting or tanking a match. Do not lie about quitting. The tactical general and the king know when you quit. They are usually much older than the player and have much more experience than the player. There's much more at stake than winning and losing a game for them. When they tell you "you quit," you quit. Expect to get punished. And remember, the punishment for surrendering or quitting was death in the past.

Importance of not surrendering – player's no-surrender character

Not only should the fighting spirit be felt by the opponent in front of you, but the people watching should feel it too, for the next time you have to battle the others. This doesn't mean that the player has to say "come on!" every time they win a point. Some players can be silent on the court, but their presence can still be felt by the opponent. It is up to the player to decide how they present themselves on the court.

Comeback victory – bigger the gap, the sweeter the victory

Until the last breath is taken, the battle is not over. No matter how badly you're being beaten, the match is not over until the last point is lost. Keep your head in the match and remember that the worse the score looks during a battle, the sweeter the victory.

The scolding king – dealing with angry and upset parents

No matter how good you are, you are going to lose battles at some point in your career. Actually, you might lose more than you'll win. There's no such thing as a draw in a battle. It's how you lose that makes the king angry. The king doesn't understand how bad it feels to lose a battle themselves. If they do know how losing feels, then they are probably angry at how you take or react to a loss. If the combat general is acting like everything is fine, there's some misunderstanding about what just happened. The loss might not be entirely the combat general's responsibility, but it is also not someone else's responsibility. It might be hard to accept, but it's yours as well, the combat general. It's difficult for a young general to take the responsibility, but they need to understand that they are the ones that are fighting in the battlefield. When the king is angry, it is best to stay silent and only answer the questions that are asked. It is best to be sincere in the answers. If you didn't show any fight or composure out on the battlefield, you can't really say anything to make the king feel better.

People get angry most of the time when they don't understand what's happening and things seem outside of their control. It's usually difficult for the combat general to see the big picture of how the battle was lost. The tactical general should evaluate and analyze what it is that a combat general could have done better and how they should have reacted to certain situations.

After the lost battle, it's not the end – analyzing and preparing for training with the coach after a loss

It's not the end of the world. The time period right after a loss determines the true character of a fighter (champion). Anyone can think and make a new plan, but it's difficult to do. Don't just think it; act and do. Talk with your tactical general to see what you could have done better and tell them what it was that was troubling you out on the battlefield. If the problem can be fixed right away, be ready to walk out onto the court right after a loss. It's the best time to work on your game.

Respecting other nations' generals – respecting the other players and their coaches

The generals from all nations should have respect for each other outside of the battlefield. The players are only hurting their own reputation if they are disrespectful to others. There are times when you'll need help. Remember that a foe today can be a friend tomorrow. It's hard to respect someone if the combat general feels like the enemy is just a private (卒 兵), but give them respect as another person and not just based on their abilities.

Shameful and dishonorable tactics – bad line calls, cheating or

mistakes?

When the opponent appears to cheat, the player has to judge if the opponent was really cheating or making mistakes. Everyone does make mistakes. Even you have made some unsure calls in your favor. If the enemy is known for their treachery and dirty tactics, then the player should get the referee to put the match on even terms. Do not get emotional and try to stay calm. If the negative energy is too much to handle, try to change it to positive energy to give yourself a mental boost. If the opponent cheats after the referee leaves or does it constantly, then give them a taste of their own medicine. Honest generals hate dirty tactics and might not feel comfortable cheating, but it's the last resort. Call the referee after you've made a bad call to prevent the opponent from cheating again.

Weapon of choice – equipment: rackets, strings, shoes, etc.

The player has to trust his equipment like a combat general trusts his weapons. Don't let anyone control your equipment. They can give you advice and recommendations, but do not give someone total control of what you should be using. Make sure you try it and battle test it, and compare the rackets and strings side by side at the same time in practice if you can.

A racket or string change is a weapon change. Just because the blacksmith (sponsors or a company) comes out with a new weapon, you don't have to switch to it right away. Make sure to test the racket thoroughly and see if you can hit the same shots as before and/or what type of shots you can add. More importantly, determine what types of shots you can't hit with it. In the *Romance of the Three Kingdoms*, combat generals have their choice of weapons and they cherish their weapons. Some generals never switch once they have a weapon that they like. It's like a trademark of a general and an element of fear for the enemy generals.

Even if your tactical general recommends a weapon change, you have to test it. The player is the one actually using it. Test it with your tactical general for him/her to check the ball speed, ball control, spin, height, depth, heaviness, and maneuverability. After the test is done in practice, battle test it. Spar. Play sets and get a feel for it. Try to get honest feedback from the opponent in a practice match (which is very difficult to get). They might not tell you the truth or even know how to explain the difference at all. It's best to discuss the effects and the feel with the tactical general, but in the end, it's up to the combat general to decide what they want to use.

Everything matters – professionalism

Habits and lifestyle are very important for a combat general. Those habits include: eating right, stretching, shadow motion, taking care of yourself, not getting injured off the court, jackets in air conditioned buildings, sleeping habits, staying fit, doing rehab, and warming up properly. It all matters in terms of your longevity and what you are fighting for. It prepares you for the unexpected and will help you prepare for an opportunity. Efforts must be made beforehand to help you be physically and mentally ready for battle. There's much at stake and many sacrifices have been made for you. You won't lose focus if you've done everything you can to prepare yourself.

Don't expect your enemies to be just as lazy as you are. They are probably ready to kill you the instant they see a weakness. They are practicing in a meaningful way when you're just having fun. They are practicing when you're taking a vacation. You may win a few battles with bad habits and an undisciplined lifestyle, but you will not win the war.

Rest and resupplying – resting is training too

Take time to enjoy other things in life. Being a tennis player is a demanding job, but it doesn't mean you have to sacrifice your entire life. Giving yourself adequate breaks is necessary and an important aspect of training. Refresh your mind and find some activities that will help you take your mind off tennis once in a while. When your mind is fresh, you can see things differently and come back even stronger than before.

Friends outside of tennis – the best friends without all the jealousy and rivalry

Try making some friends outside of your tennis life, if possible. Most of your tennis friends are also your rivals. Even though your friends outside of tennis can't relate to your sport, they can help you relax and take your mind off all the battles and wars you've been through. If the friend plays a different sport, they can understand and relate to some of the issues you're having, so it's great to have a friend that understands the troubles you're going through. Being in similar situations and being able to relate to someone has a very positive impact on your mental health.

I want to rule all the nations one day, be the king – becoming pro and working to be number 1

You have to be ready to work for it. It's easy for anyone to say they are going to rule the world, but there is more than just wanting it. You have to live it and show it. Dream big, but set realistic goals and conquer them one by one. All the work you've done in the past will help you to become the new king. You'll have to make all the decisions yourself when you become the king. The former king can give you advice, but ultimately you'll be responsible for your actions. When your parents pass on the throne to you, it's not the end—it's a new beginning.

The combat general's most powerful weapon is not the ability to play or to hit amazing shots. The most powerful weapons for the combat general are a strong mentality (firm but flexible), love of the sport, and self-management to be ready for an opportunity. It is difficult for a young warrior to have all of these traits, but they can all be developed through hard work.

SECTION 2

*Understanding
the Art of Professional Tennis*

The book *The Art of War* has made me realize as a pro tennis player how important tennis was in my life. It might be just a game for some, but for pros, it's like a never-ending war. Not only do you have to battle opponents and the world, but battling the loneliness of being a pro tennis player takes its toll. Even after all the struggles, there comes a time when you start enjoying the gruesome and cruel nature of this sport and the feeling of being a lone warrior going into battle. That feeling that no one can say anything to you and the world outside can be forgotten is priceless for anyone that plays this sport. And the high you get when victory is achieved cannot be matched by any other game. You'll soon be brought back down by another loss, but then there comes a point where the pain becomes dull and the losses only help you to improve, to reach new heights.

This section is written to help players and parents understand the game of tennis—from the point system to the environment that the players have to use. This section will use Sun Tzu's *The Art of War* for comparing tennis to warfare. There are 13 chapters in *The Art of War*: Initial Calculations (計), Waging War (作戰), Plan of Attack (謀攻), Physical Disposition (形), Form of Power (勢), Weaknesses and Strengths (虛實), Military Maneuvers (軍爭), Variations and Adaptations (九變), Movement of the Army (行軍), Terrain (地形), Nine Battlegrounds (九地), Attacking with Fire (火攻), and Intelligence and Espionage (用間). All of the chapters are closely related to each other and the subject matter might seem to jump around from one topic to another, but just like in warfare as a whole, the mind of a tennis player must be rock solid but also flexible and creative at the same time. The sections within the chapters that are irrelevant to tennis will be omitted to make it easier to understand for tennis players. Some of the material might overlap with what is covered in the first section: Understanding the Team.

Importance of fundamentals and technique

Sun Tzu does not talk about how well a general has to be able to physically fight, but the generals in the past were all masters of some form of martial arts and a weapon of choice, and they were able to kill the enemies with their skills. Tennis is also much like martial arts in the sense that a player beginning to learn the fundamentals and the proper way to play cannot beat a player that knows how to win with unconventional technical skill and with more experience in actual match play. As time goes by, there is a very slim chance of a professionally trained player losing to a weekend player, comparable to a master of martial arts losing to a street brawler without any training. It might be difficult for a beginning tennis player to use their technique and shots until they can fully execute without much thought, just as a person learning how to master a technique in martial arts must take time to be able to land a shot in an actual fight. Different types of situations require adapting and using different techniques and skills to execute an attack or to defend an attack. Learning and gaining experience takes time, and most people do not have the patience and the discipline to learn all of the skills and techniques properly, and they give up and try to improve their game without proper training. In order for a player to be able to use various strategies and tactics, they must be fundamentally solid and be able to execute the shots. Without the fundamentals, these strategies and tactics are as good as garbage.

I.

INITIAL CALCULATIONS (計) – PLANNING AHEAD

This section is about the importance of initial preparations before war. The emphasis is on how precise and accurate the overall plans have to be in order to achieve victory. In tennis, it can be translated into how the parents or the players (when they are mature enough to be their own leader) have to manage and lead themselves toward achieving their own goals by thinking, assessing, and comparing the five fundamental factors.

There are five fundamental factors that the parents/kings have to consider for the best probability of success, the ways (道), seasons (天時), terrain (地), leadership (將), and management (法). These can be translated into ethics and morals, timing and seasons (weather), environmental (physical) factors, coach's capacity and ability, and relationship between the team and financial backing. The leaders must be able to check and solve these issues if there is a problem with any of them before the war begins. In addition to the five major factors, there are seven questions that help analyze the quality of the team. The seven questions help everyone understand the readiness of the team by questioning the preparation of the equipment, quality of the training, the ability of the player, and other factors.

An initial calculation should be made by the parents with the help of the coaches and by learning from other parents that have experience developing their children into competitive tennis players at a high level. The parents can learn from other parents' mistakes and achievements. When the role of the leader changes to the player, the player has to assess and compare with the help of their coach.

a) War decides the fate of life and death

> *"Deciding to go into war is a significant and important decision. It's a matter of life and death, success or collapse, so it has to be carefully analyzed and inspected."*

[Translation]

It is easy to see and understand why one nation must take caution when going into war. It is not as easily seen or understood how difficult and damaging it can be for a family to decide to have their child play tennis at the professional level when people on the team do not understand what it takes. Sun Tzu viewed warfare as not only a matter of the state, but as something that was vital to the livelihoods of the public. If the war is lost, then the livelihoods of the public will be in chaos. The foundations of their lives will be torn down. This can be translated into the livelihood of the tennis player and their family for the rest of their life. When a family decides to take that path, they are filled with hope and light. The outcome of the efforts will have a positive or a negative effect on their life. Because of these reasons, Sun Tzu has stressed the importance of checking the five major factors. If the five factors are not supplied, then the war cannot be won.

The attention to the phrase should be about the analysis as a whole. It is very important to look at things from a third-person perspective. Being able to analyze the situations and the world is key. The analysis can be misjudged if one cannot look at themselves and analyze themselves truthfully. Having confidence and financial assets are important, but there are many other factors that can decide the outcome. Some parents are not able to see past the limitations of their own child. The belief that their child can make it is great, but the calculations have to be based on some experience in the field and in professional sports. "A collapsed nation cannot re-exist and the dead cannot be revived." The decision cannot be based on justification or to show off to others. There are success stories told by the top pros and their parents, but there are countless other stories of the ones that have tried but were not as successful. They are not spoken of, as if it has never happened before, much like the existence of the collapsed nations in history.

b) Five factors to understand before going into war

> *"So it should be managed by considering the five major factors and by answering the seven questions to investigate the situation. The first factor are the Ways (道), second factor is the seasons (天), third factor is the terrain (地), fourth factor is the leadership (將), and the fifth factor is management(法).*
>
> *The Ways are how the people and the leader's mind and goals are equal to one another. If they have one mind and are united, the people will follow the leader without any doubts even if it is a matter of life or death. The people will not be afraid of the dangers that lie in front of them. Seasons relates to the dark and lighted areas, cold and hot temperature, and the changing seasons in a year. Terrain are the distance of land, rough or flat, wide and narrow, and the zones of life or death. Leadership are the wisdom (智), faith (信), righteousness (仁), bravery (勇), and discipline (嚴). Management means the form of the military, rewards and punishment, and food supply. These five factors must be heard by the leader. Leader who take these into account can be victorious, and the leader who does not cannot win."*

[Translation]

It is imperative to examine these five factors that decide the outcome of war. Although only five words, it may be fairly said that these factors sum up everything about warfare. In tennis, the five factors can be translated into:

Ways (道) =	The parents and player having the same dream, mindset, and goals.
Seasons (天) =	The overall timing and flow, shadows and light, day and night, altitude, temperature, and the climate of the region of training and tournaments.
Terrain (地) =	The distance between training area and home, distance between home and the tournaments, the surface of the court, and the zones of the court.
Leadership (將) =	The leaders' (mostly the coach but can also be parents, or pro player) wisdom, faith, righteousness, guts, and self-discipline.
Management (法) =	Distinct roles of the team (parents, coach, and players), rewards and punishment, and finances.

It is said that if these factors are thoroughly examined, players can play at their maximum potential and the benefits of the coach's plans and strategies can be fully utilized. The matters of seasons, terrain, and management can be seen relatively easily, even for the inexperienced, but the ways and leadership need to be closely examined because they deal with the relationship between people and the team itself. The relationships between the people and the team are far more important than any other factors.

The parents and the coach have to have the same dream, will, and goals as the player and be compassionate to be able to lead a developing player. During the career, the players need to be able to have faith and respect for their parents and coach. In order for this to happen, the parents and coach must be good role models. It is extremely important to have a healthy relationship between the parents, coach, and the player.

c) Seven calculations to measure the team's capacity and abilities

"So the seven questions has to be answered to compare and measure the probability of wins and losses. The seven questions are;

First, which king keeps and are able to conduct their Ways?
Second, which general is more capable?
Third, who has the seasons (weather and timing) and terrain?
Fourth, is law and order strictly enforced?
Fifth, who has a stronger military strength?
Sixth, which military has been better trained?
Seven, are the rewards and punishments clearly given at the right moment?

Based on these principles I (Sun Tzu) can estimate the probability of wins and losses of war.

If my calculations and plans are heard and used victory is certain, but if it is not heard and the military is used, one will collapse and so I will leave him."

[Translation]

When Sun Tzu met his king for the first time, he gave his king the definition of the seven questions that have to be answered in order to be able to compare and measure the probability of victory and defeat. He told the king that if the king needed him, he would stay. What is important is that the calculations and questions make it possible to estimate the physical and psychological factors. The seven questions break down the five factors in the previous section with more specific detail.

In tennis, it can be translated into these factors:

1. Do the parents (mother and father) truly have the same dreams and goals for their player? Do the parents have the same dreams and goals as the player?
2. Does the player have athletic talent and potential for tennis (hand-eye coordination, foot speed, base endurance, base strength, base reaction speed, strong mentality, sharp mind, perseverance, killer instincts, work ethic, strong body that is not injury prone, etc.)?
3. Does the player have access to a good training environment? Is the weather a limiting or a positive factor for training?
4. Does the team (parents, coach, player) have good self-discipline and order? If not, is discipline enforced?
5. What are the players' weapons and strengths? Are they overpowering and exceptional?
6. Is the player well trained (shot making/technique, endurance, self-discipline, tactics, improvisation skills, etc.)?
7. Are there any rewards and punishments for the wins and losses or results of an action (losses are measured by the performance and the attitude of the match, not an actual loss of the match)?

A nation is judged by the acts and morals of the king. A great nation is led by a great leader with good morals, and a happy family is led by a wise and caring head of household. As it is with great nations and happy families, in tennis, the leaders of the team, parents, must be able to have the same goals and dreams for their player. The player as a child will be able to dream and make goals according to their parents' dreams and morals because the parents have influence on their child. Building and guiding your child to have dreams is a great way to build self-motivation and a strong mentality. Just as in a nation where the military needs to believe in their king to be able to fight fearlessly, the child not only needs to believe in their own dreams but the dreams of their parents as well. The morals and the respectability of their parents will help build a strong-minded tennis player as they develop into a mature warrior on the court. If the parents lack respectability and faith in their child, the player can surrender to the opponents, or worse, they can give up on their tennis career. If the parents lack faith in their child, the child will get confused and will not have anywhere to go. When the goals and dreams become one, the player will be able to endure the hardships of a tennis player and the tough training.

The morals and the dreams of the parents are very important to a coach as well as themselves (parents and player). The parents might not be able to answer and measure the differences in the seven questions. In order for someone to be able to analyze these natural and artificial factors accurately, they must be keen on seeing the matter macroscopically and microscopically. Since the parents are not able to accurately estimate these factors, they need a coach to be able to counsel them truthfully and transparently. If the parents are not very understanding, then the coach will not be able to remonstrate truthfully, thus rendering the coach's ability useless. As much as the parents have power and control over who they can hire as a coach, the coach also has a choice of which parents they will work with. Ancient war strategist and descendant of Sun Tzu, Sun Bin, said, *"if you have not met a great king, do not work for any king."* When parents and players hire a coach, they need to remember that an experienced coach is very careful about choosing which parents and players they will work with.

The most common mistakes are related to the fourth and the seventh question. The question that needs to be answered is how the responsibilities will be assigned to the parents, coach, and the player. This is very important because of how much love the parents have for the player/child. If the love for the child is expressed with extreme kindness and soft-heartedness or parents insist on retaining all authority, even on the court, then order and discipline cannot be adequately maintained. This is devastating for the relationship among team members because the coach has to be able to discipline the player to the point where the parents might not be able to justify the coach's actions. It is extremely tough for the parents to see someone other than themselves punish and discipline their child. As this is tough and heartbreaking to see, the parents might want to do discipline their child themselves. But when the player and coach are on the court, the coach needs total respect from the player to be able to train them properly. The player needs to have a sense of respect and loyalty for the coach when tennis is involved. The coach has to have total authority and when instructions are given, it is not to be taken lightly. The parents stepping in while the coach is in the act of disciplining or training the player is probably the worst action the parents can take since the player will have a sense of comfort and protection over the coach's actions. When the coach's respect is compromised, the young player will unconsciously place themselves higher than their coach. When this happens, clear instructions cannot be given to the player because the player will not follow the coach if the training is too tough or hard to understand.

The parents must know that the coaches have good reasons for acting stubborn and fierce. Once the coach loses the respect of their player, the coach loses their power and the ability to instruct the player. The parents must be wise and well-tempered to be able to judge what is best for their player in the long run.

So where is the fun? And why is it not in the seven calculations for a developing competitive tennis player? The fun comes from the parents and the coach's ability to lead, improving their game or adding shots to their game, making their shots feel cleaner, and the high a player gets when winning a match, game, or tournament. Fun can be a major factor in the initial stages of developing a tennis player, but actual "fun" is not a huge factor for succeeding at the developmental stage when the vision, dream, and faith takes over a player. The thought of achieving their dreams and positive reinforcement and guidance should be exciting enough to keep them self-motivated. When the player is working for their dreams, they should know that working hard pays off months and years later. It is very important for the young player to have access to high-level tennis and an intense environment at a young age to learn from the older and better players and see how tough and intense their training needs to be. As the child is not mature enough to fully understand, it is the parents' job to help their player by rewarding them when they work hard to achieve their goals and inculcate a strong work ethic. The war begins way before they start playing tennis. The positive reinforcements of hopes and dreams need to be made by the child's parents in order for them to be able to stay positive and strong minded throughout their career.

d) Strategy and tactics = deception

> *"If my stratagems benefits are understood, it will be advantageous for the disposition of the military (形) and the form of power(勢) can be shifted in form to favor the military.*
>
> *All warfare is based on deception (詭道). Therefore, even if capable you have to appear incapable to the enemy, be strategic and tactical but appear to be unplanned to the enemy, when aiming somewhere close make it seem like you're aiming far, when aiming far make it seem like you're aiming close to the enemy.*
>
> *Make it seem like it's advantageous for the enemy to lure them and confuse them internally to launch a surprise attack. If the enemy is firm then defend, if the enemy is strong avoid them, if the enemy is outraged then disturb them, if the enemy is cowardly make them feel over confident, if the enemy is comfortable then make them work, if two enemies have joined forces then make them turn on each other. Attack where the enemy is unprepared and sortie to where it is unthinkable. These are the ways to be victorious in war, so it must not be revealed beforehand."*

[Translation]

Tennis is a game of deception. Just by looking closely at the players' actions and words, people can get a good sense that tennis is a deceptive sport. Saying sorry or holding up a hand to signal to the opponent that they are sorry when they win a point by a let court. Saying good match to each other even when the score of the match is won single sided. Bad line calls. Saying come on with a fist pump when you know you've missed a shot to see if your opponent would call the ball in. The actions and shot selections of the player also have to be deceptive. Hitting the ball to the open court most of the time, then on a big point, going behind the opponent to tie your opponent's feet, luring your opponents to hit to the open court to make them hit to your strength, backing up behind the baseline acting like you're going to hit deep heavy ball, but hitting heavy short angle to catch the opponent off guard, acting like you're going to hit a big approach shot on a short ball, but hitting a drop shot. The similarities between warfare and tennis cannot be ignored.

The fighting power of the military is not defined by the raw firepower a military has. Although very advantageous and it adds another dimension to being able to be deceptive, a player's ability or the fighting power is not only defined by the raw power and the quality of the shots being hit. The point is that the form of power (形勢) is the style (形) that a player plays and the shot selection (勢) can be changed according to different opponents to play the match favorably for the player.

e) The probability of victory

"Predicting victory in the strategy room before the war means that there's plenty of deceptive tactics (妙策) at ones disposal, if one thinks that the outcome of war will not lead to victory it is because there's not enough deceptive tactics. Abundant tactics equal supremacy and lack of tactics equal inferiority. So how can you not have a plan!

Based on these principles and observations, I can surely see victory or defeat."

[Translation]

Calculating the probability of a win starts before the actual battle or war. If the five factors to consider and the seven calculations help estimate a successful player at a larger scale, the probability of victory deals with the estimates to calculate the outcome of a match. Deceptive tactics (妙策) in tennis have to be carried out throughout the whole match, not just one point, game, or set. Being able to execute those tactics requires lots of technical work, self-discipline, and experience on the court. This is the reason why, at a young age, building a technical foundation is so important. It is not because hitting great shots and having perfect form is so important; it is because the players need to be able to execute the tactics properly and easily, and hide their patterns of play to leave adequate room for their brain to execute the tactics, reading their opponent's tactics, and using their environment to their advantage. When focusing on how to hit the ball "in" at a stage where one needs to think about strategy and tactics, they will struggle to execute the strategy and tactics, making tennis a very difficult and boring game of pong.

Style of play can be easily seen by anyone who's watched someone practice or plays a match, but the shot selection of a player and the form of power (勢) cannot be easily seen. This is the reason why most parents without any tennis background cannot teach the game as the game gets more complex and the success and mistakes in the match cannot be easily seen. Most tennis parents focus on either the technical aspect of the game or the strategical aspect of the game. Some coaches make these mistakes as well and this is where the distinction between a beginner coach and an elite professional coach comes into play. Sun Tzu states that Physical Disposition (形) and the Form of Power (勢) are very closely related and cannot be measured as to which is more important. It is also true in tennis that the basic style of play and tendencies of a player are very closely related to the shot selection and it is nearly impossible to determine which is more important because one benefits from the other.

Although playing many tournaments can help a prepared player, an unprepared player trying to gain experience by playing tournaments without any purpose can lead to loss of confidence. A player cannot win every tournament they participate in, but when playing a tournament, the player should have a purpose like gaining experience by working on specific tactics or techniques in a tournament to test and to break through their nerves to actually use a technique or tactic in a match. If the player is not trained enough to have a purpose to gain experience through a match, the coach can stop the parents/king and opt to not play the tournament. It is not because the coach is afraid of losing their job because of a loss, but it is because the outcome can be clearly seen by the coach through these calculations, and it would not be beneficial for an unprepared player to go out and play a tournament. Note that probability of victory is only for the tactician/coach to consider. The general/player needs to fight fearlessly once the battle starts no matter what the circumstances.

II.

WAGING WAR (作戰) – IMPORTANCE OF FINANCES AND RESOURCES AND MAINTAINING MORALE ON THE ROAD

The literal translation of 作戰 means construction (作) of battle (戰). Although the two Chinese characters put together to form a word can also mean strategy at a smaller scale (match level), this chapter is about how to manage the overall operations of the military. The importance of managing the rations and supplies and resources and finances of a military is critical. The rations and supplies will be interpreted as the players' fitness and mental health. The resources and finances will be interpreted as the funding capacity of the parents. Most parents manage their finances very poorly and spend their resources either carelessly or too carefully. Finding a balance is not easy and because it is not easy, it's better to have more rather than less. Although abundant is better than limited, spending the resources wisely is definitely better than having abundant resources. An army that's too big means more expenses and the rate at which the expenses are spent is faster. Not only that, if there are siblings involved and the parents spend expenses on a child that is trying to go pro and the other children and husband/wife cannot afford anything, then there will be lots of complaints. This chapter should help parents, coaches, and players understand how important finances and resources are and keeping the players physically and mentally healthy to keep the team's morale high.

a) Calculate the expenses

> *"The principles of moving the military is to be able to have a thousand light carts and a thousand heavy wagons transport rations over 1000 li (200 miles). Expenses towards national and international matters, entertainment expenses for nation's guests, gluing materials, and supplies to maintain the carts and armors deplete a thousand silvers a day. Only when these expenses can be covered can you move a 100,000 men."*

[Translation]

National power, in other words, is economic power. A nation cannot afford to go to war with other nations without economic power. No matter how wealthy a nation is, it is true that a nation has to be ready to spend an enormous sum of money. As the player develops, the player can have a team of experts travel with them. Coach, physical trainers, doctors, managers, nutritionist, mental trainer, stringers, and other important people. The parents have to spend wisely to choose what their child needs. Having an unnecessarily big team is not always the answer.

Spending the right amount of money at the right time is key. The most common mistake that I've encountered is not investing enough in physical trainers. Physical trainers are able to keep the player performing at the optimal level throughout their travels and training periods. In order for the player to stay physically healthy (rehab) and maintain their performance level, an expert is needed. Remember that when the experts are hired for travels, fee per day or whatever x amount of days from first day of travel to last day of travel, meals, drinks, hotel, transportation, entertainment expenses, and the potential loss of income while traveling has to be covered.

Guan Zhong, who was the Prime Minister of Qi in 720 BC in Chinese history, said that, *"ones' storage has to be filled with goods to get a good sense of manners and etiquette, and when the cost of living is fulfilled one forms moral consciousness."* He has also said, *"if the resources are not plentiful, it is not mentally possible to lead a nation."* This can translate to how the parents spend their resources. If the parents are not financially stable to support a developing player, then it is not possible to be a graceful and classy leader. All the financial resources spent on various things will be stressful and the stress will lead to misjudgment and bad decisions. The stress will also be felt by everyone who is making an effort to help the player.

b) Dragging on a match can lead to defeat

> *"When you engage in actual fighting, if victory is long in coming, then the men's weapons will get blunt and their fighting spirit will diminish. Attacking a castle at this state will only waste the armies' energy. When the battle is protracted, a nation's resources will get insufficient. When the weapons get blunt, fighting spirit low, energy exhausted, and resources spent, other feudal lords will take advantage of the troubles. Then even the wisest man cannot handle the consequences. Thus in war tactics and strategy, "imperfect but fighting swiftly and intensively to bring to an end (速戰速決)" may have been used but cunningly slow and dragging on the battle has not. Thus, one who cannot understand all the unfavorable odds, they cannot know all the favorable odds."*

[Translation]

Although preparations before the war have to be thoroughly examined, once the battle starts, fighting must be done swiftly and intensively to end the battle efficiently. In tennis, this can be applied in two ways.

The first way it can be applied is when the player is actually playing a match. The match must not be allowed to drag on and must be finished as soon as possible to prevent from losing too much energy and stamina. This is very important because there is no time limit governing the match as a whole, so if a match drags on, fatigue from the previous match can carry over to the next. Although if the player was trained properly during the non-competition period, the player should not be getting too tired, it is best to keep the matches as short as possible to have enough energy and to keep the body somewhat fresh to be able to win the tournament. It does not mean to conserve energy to defeat the opponent but to be decisive when there's a chance to win the point, the player should take an advantage right away and try to find the best tactics and strategies to defeat the opponent in the shortest amount of time. They should never confuse this as conserving energy, the meaning of 速戰速決 is to fight swiftly and intensively, not cunningly slow. Although there are different ways to attack on the court, when the opportunity arises to attack, the player should attack.

The second way to apply this to tennis is in the quote *"..., if victory is long in coming, then the men's weapons will get blunt and their fighting spirit will diminish... When the battle is protracted, a nation's resources will get insufficient...."* This can apply when the player is traveling to tournaments for weeks and sometimes months; their training from the non-competition period will slowly wear off. The traveling player's fighting spirit diminishes as the weeks pass, and staying away from home will lead to low energy levels physically and mentally. The nation's resources can relate to the parents or the family's financial state. The longer the duration the player travels, the more funds it will take to sustain the player's level throughout the travels. This can mean that traveling with a coach or physical trainers takes almost double if not more than double the funds. The budget must be calculated and limited, and the travels should end before the expenses are too difficult to be recovered.

c) Fitness training at the tournament

> *"One that is proficient in war tactics does not need to recruit a second wave of militia and does not move the rations and supplies three times in the same battle. Although the resources can be brought from home, the rations and supplies are fulfilled by taking them from the enemy."*

[Translation]

At that time, if the rations and supplies could be obtained from the enemy, the costs could be significantly reduced. Managing rations was one of the most important issues to solve in warfare. Since the food supply is not relevant in recent times, this section relates rations and supplies to the players' fitness level and mental health.

When traveling for ITF junior tournaments or pro tournaments, players will be on the road several weeks at a time. It is not economical to have the player travel from a tournament, then back home to rejuvenate, then go back on the road to a different tournament in the span of a week or two. Traveling back and forth will exhaust the player more than rejuvenate them. It is best to perform physical training and rehabilitation on the road with a trainer.

To keep a player mentally healthy, it is good to find things to do in the area in between the tournaments to relax the players. Pro players usually know how to relax and can find things to do. As a junior, the coach or parents can help the player by finding fun things to do to keep their mind and body healthy and motivated without wasting too much energy. It does not necessarily have to be finding fun things to do, but if the players have been traveling outside of their home country for a while, eating a good meal from back home can also rejuvenate a player.

d) The cost of traveling and training

> *"The reason why a nation can be led to poverty is because the military supplies has to be transported a great distance. When the military supplies are transported a great distance the citizens will get struck with poverty.*
>
> *If the military is positioned near a town, the prices of goods will inflate and when inflation happens citizens' finances will be depleted. When finances are depleted, the citizens will be afflicted by heavy exactions. With exhaustion of strength, loss of finances, the central town district will be deserted and the citizens income will be cut by seven-tenths (70%). While the government expenses for broken chariots, worn out horses, breast-plates, helmets, bow and arrow, spears and shields, draught-oxen and heavy wagons, will amount to six-tenths (60%) of total revenue."*

[Translation]

Without any rations and resources, the military cannot hold out or move into the enemy's territory. As the distance between home and an enemy territory increases, it takes more rations and resources to move the military. As the player moves into the higher levels, they will have to travel farther away from home to participate in bigger events. The farther away the tournament is from home, the more time and money it takes to support them.

The second part of the quote can relate to how much money it takes even when the player is training at home. In order for the player to be getting the right training, it takes a huge chunk of the parents' finances. Below are some basic calculations done without expenses spent on anything other than tennis.

Private lessons of minimum 2 times a week,
average lesson fee of $80 x 2 =$160 per week
Physical training minimum of 3 times a week,
average lesson fee of $80 x 3 = $240 per week
1 month 3-4 hour academy sessions each day for 5 days a week = $1200
A month of tennis training expenses without doctors,
transportation expenses, time lost driving, and other expenses = $2800

Average US income for median household in 2013
= $51,939 per year and $4,328.25 per month

$2800 spent on tennis per month / $4328.25 average US income per month = 65% of total income per month

The calculations can vary, but the rough estimates turn out to be 60-70% of the total income for an average household. There are ways to save money, but this would be a typical amount parents would spend if a junior player is attending a tennis academy and the parents do not have any time to feed balls to the players themselves. The price indicated for the academy is the bare minimum and usually costs upwards rather than downwards. The price is an estimate of only afternoon sessions and it takes more money to attend both morning and afternoon sessions. The $80 set for a private lesson with a tennis coach is an average cost, which means that it's for an average coach. The price set for directors and head coaches might run even higher. The above calculations do not include any academics, cost of playing local tournaments, and other expenses of raising a child or other siblings. Hiring a private coach to work with a player is much more costly than attending an academy with private lessons. When hiring a private coach, a physical trainer is also recommended, and hotels, food, and other accommodations have to be paid by the parents. If the player is good enough to get sponsored for training and travels, the parents need to save the funds in case the player gets the sponsorship taken away. Whatever the reason may be for getting the sponsorship taken away (due to drop in ranking, injuries, or attitude or conduct), the player must be able to travel and train without a sponsor.

e) Rewards and prize money

> "So in order to kill the enemy, our men must be made to feel strong hostility towards the enemy. Our men fight to capture the enemy's properties because they get rewarded with the properties captured from the enemy. Therefore, in chariot fighting, when more than ten chariots have been taken, the one who captured the first chariot is rewarded. The flag on the captured chariot is replaced with the flag of our own and used with our other chariots and the captured soldiers should be treated kindly and trained to be one of our own. This is called, the more victories you achieve the stronger you get."

[Translation]

The psychological tactics to capture the enemy's resources and the use of the resources have been quoted. In warfare, it was very important to use the captured resources and incorporate them into one's own army. Not only was it important to physically add power to an army, but the psychological effects of rewarding the soldiers were significant as they were able to gain motivation and fighting spirit.

Unless there's a sponsor to support a players' training and travels, the parents spend their money for the expenses and when a player wins a tournament and receives prize money, the parents might feel like they deserve to keep the prize money, but parents should reward the player by letting the player keep or spend a part of the prize money they have earned. The best way to spend the prize money is to use it for the expenses for upcoming tournaments, but if the parents can reward the players, it can give a significant mental boost for the player.

III.

PLAN OF ATTACK (謀攻) – INTRODUCTION TO THE OVERALL STRATAGEM OF ATTACK

This chapter is the last part of the introduction, which includes Initial Calculations and Waging War. The character 謀 can be translated into many meanings. Tricky, cunning, sly, and artful can be used to translate the character 謀. The character 攻 means to attack. When the two characters are put together, it means artful attack. Although this chapter is tied in closely with the first two chapters, it feels as though this is the introduction and lays the foundation for the next three chapters: Disposition of the Military(形), Form of Power(勢), and Weaknesses and Strengths(虛實). The actual context in this chapter focuses on the overall plans of how to attack by knowing yourself and your enemy.

It is also very important to know oneself and the opponent in tennis. Before any strategy can be deployed, the player needs to know what they are capable of and know how the opponent will react to your moves. By knowing oneself, it is possible to make plans for how to defeat your opponent in their own ways. Many of the junior years before becoming a challenger-level pro are spent determining what is possible and what is not possible to use as strategies or tactics. Some of the strategies and tactics that are useful in the juniors do not work in the pros because they are simply too obvious or the shot itself is not good enough to pressure the opponent. Among other things, developing the right tools to employ the right strategy at the higher level is key to becoming a top level pro tennis player.

a) Win without fighting

> *"Generally, it is best to conquer an enemy nation as a whole and intact; it is second best to shatter and destroy the enemy's nation. It is best to capture an entire division (12,500 men) rather than to destroy it. It is also best to capture battalions (500 men), company (100-500 men), and platoons (5-100 men) rather than to destroy them. So it is said that to fight the enemy and conquering them in all your battles is not supreme excellence; supreme excellence consists in breaking the enemy's resistance without fighting."*

[Translation]

The best way to conquer is to keep whatever the enemy has intact. In other words, it is best to use as little resources as possible to be efficient when conquering the enemy. It might be difficult to directly translate it into tennis, but when a player plays a match at a tournament, it is very important to be efficient. The player needs to keep their stamina intact as much as they can while beating the opponent at the moment. When the best strategy is to keep the points short, the player should keep the points short; when the best strategy is to keep it consistent, then the player should try to keep the points as long as possible to break their opponents.

Winning without fighting in tennis means trying to make the opponent look bad by making them do what they don't like to do on the court. Some players love pace and when pace is given, they can dictate on the court, but when slower or heavy topspin is given to them, they might try to end the point too early and miss a ton of easy balls. On the other end, some players might like to keep the points long and will try to push or hit moon balls to keep the point going on forever so that their opponent gets tired and impatient. Although using your best shots to fight and win the match is great, it might take more mental and physical effort to break them down with only the big guns. The best way to win is by taking away the opponent's weapons and strengths to win matches. In order for a player to do this, they have to learn to hit various shots and make correct shot selections.

This is the reason why, at the top level, it is best to start the match with Plan B (slightly second best to the A game) unless the players have played each other multiple times and know each other very well . When playing matches with their average match play style, instead of their best style, they are not easily showing their opponents what they can do and, at the same time, they are getting the feel of their opponents' strengths and weaknesses, watching the opponents' moves by analyzing the patterns and shots being hit in certain types of situations. If the Plan B is working and is effectively beating the opponent, then their Plan A is hidden until they need it in big points. If Plan B wasn't good enough and the set was barely lost, then the player can change strategies according to the first set and use their A game to start their counterattack in the second set. Plans A and B are loose terms, and the plans are broken down into small tactics based on certain situations at the higher level. This method takes lots of experience and open mind in the match to be able to analyze correctly and does not work when the opponent is at a much higher level than the player.

Juniors and amateurs usually play their match with their A game first; then they don't have any game style to fall back on since their B game is just pushing (hitting the ball back with low pace) or their B game is not developed enough to be used in a match. While it is very important to keep developing their style of play (Chapter 4 – Military Disposition), it is also important to develop shot selection and tactics (Chapter 5 – Form of Power) according to their opponents. It is important to hit big and develop guts and nerves early to be able to fight head-on with their opponents, but as the level gets higher, it is crucial to be able to hide their weapons, deceive their opponents, make the opponents play into their strengths, and be able to change their tactics and styles according to their opponents.

In other words, do not try to fight the opponent by playing into the opponents strengths. Win without fighting by exploiting their weaknesses and letting your opponent break down on their own. The goal is to win the match, not to measure who has better shots.

b) Besieging the enemy's castle – taking down a pusher/defensive player

> *"Thus the highest form of generalship is to balk the enemy's plans; the next is to end their allegiance with their allies; the next in order is to attack the enemy's army in the field; and the worst policy of all is to besiege the walled castles and cities. Assaulting and besieging a castle should only be done when there is no other choice. The preparation of mobile shelters and siege tanks, and various implements of war will take up three whole months and the piling up of mounds against walls will take three additional months. A general unable to control his irritation will launch his men to the assault like swarming ants, with the result that has one-third of his men slain, while the castle still remains untaken. Such are the disastrous effects of a siege.*
>
> *Therefore a skillful general forces surrender from enemy troops without fighting, captures castles without laying siege to them, and overthrows their kingdom without lengthy operations in the field. With his practical ingenuity by keeping his forces intact he will dispute the mastery of the Empire. This is the method of attacking the walls by stratagem."*

[Translation]

The priority of attack is attacking the enemy's plans (伐謀), attacking their alliance (伐交), attacking their army (伐兵), then attacking their castle (攻城). There are more sacrifices made and fewer returns as it goes down the list. Although it is sometimes impossible to avoid battles in war, Sun Tzu express three "don'ts": Don't fight (非戰), Don't attack (非攻), and Don't prolong (非久), which are based on his tactics to be very psychological. The point here is that besieging a castle or the town walls leads to huge sacrifices on the part of the generals' army.

In tennis, there are very defensive players (like a wall) all throughout the levels, from beginner to pro level. Unless there's a clear level difference from the defensive player, the player playing the defensive player can never expect an easy match. It takes accurate placement, self-discipline, and lots of patience to wait for the right ball to attack or to create an opportunity to attack. Like a strategy in warfare, it might also be smart to have the defensive player come out of the castle walls. If the player is fast enough and if their ability allows it, it might be a good strategy to force the defensive player to attack and counterattack back to surprise them. Unless the players' level is higher than the defensive player, asking a player to go all-out aggressive (which is misunderstood by most developing juniors and amateurs to hit big) on an equally leveled defensive player is like asking them to go out on the battlefield and kill themselves. The coach can ask the young player to play an all-out offensive style, but this is for developing their future game, not because this is an efficient strategy (it might be the only strategy for a player that's not crafty enough). The players need to learn when to attack and when not to attack by trial and error. When watching this type of match, it is very important for the coaches and parents to stay calm even if the player makes a mistake. It will give the young player a chance to realize for themselves what they are doing. If the coach or parents are too emotional on every shot they hit, then it is very difficult for the young player to think for themselves on the court and it significantly slows down the learning process of analyzing themselves properly. Talking to them about the match after the match is much more effective rather than showing all the negative emotions while the player is playing a match.

c) Rules of engagement

> "It is the rule in war, if our forces are ten to the enemy's one, to surround them; if five to one, to attack them; if twice as numerous, to disperse the enemy. If equally matched, battle against them; if slightly inferior in numbers, we can flee from the enemy; if we are not strong enough to confront the enemy then we should avoid the enemy. Hence, if an obstinate fight may be made by a small force, in the end it will get captured by the larger force."

[Translation]

Like the last section on attacking the opponent all-out (hitting big shots), you can leave openings like losing balance after a shot, bad court positioning while trying to be too aggressive, or even making too many unforced errors. Notice when our troops are outnumbering the enemy 10 to 1, meaning the level difference is great from one player to another in tennis, the player does not need to recklessly attack on every shot and sacrifice points by making unforced errors. Surrounding the enemy does not mean attacking them; it means cornering them and watching their every move and just capturing them as a whole without making unnecessary sacrifices of our troops. When watching a match with a player at a much higher level than the other player, sometimes the higher level player doesn't look like they are so good because of this reason. Do not get fooled by what they are doing on the court with a weak opponent. They might not be as offensive because they don't need to waste energy and make unforced errors when the match can be won comfortably. The higher level player might hit a couple of great shots throughout the match, but might be hiding their true weapons and defensive skills until it is required to use all of their skills and power. Also, when the higher level player can defend or counter attack the opponent's every weapon or strength, it does not really give the opponent a chance to win. They'll feel hopeless and the match will be given to the higher level player fairly easily.

When the players seem like they are fairly equal in their levels, having a good strategy to beat them is key to winning. Offering the enemy a battle means to not only fight and grind, but it means that the player should have a strategy or need to find ways to win by using a stratagem. As players' levels start to even out, the use of tactics and strategies gets more important than ever.

Fleeing and avoiding the enemy should be understood as avoiding or neutralizing the opponents' strength as much as possible. There's a very well-known tactic: "offense is the best defense"; this strategy can apply as well when the opponents are too good to battle straight on, and using patterns and tactics to beat the opponent will not work when the opponents' level is higher than the player and all of the shots hit are being read by the opponent. This tactic can relate to suppressive fire or covering fire that degrades the performance of an enemy force to neutralize or suppress them in the military.

Obstinate fighting means to play stubbornly by playing the same way the player plays any opponent by using a comfortable method or by using strategies or tactics that are not hurting the opponent at all, but implementing them to break the opponent down. Taking chances and playing slightly recklessly at times might be the best way to beat an opponent that's at a higher level than the player, rather than playing it safe or using tactics that are very obvious to the opponent.

d) Three generals' matters the king should not get involved in

"A general is the bulwark of the State. If the bulwark is meticulous then the State will be strong, if the bulwark is damaged then the State will be weak. There are three ways in which the king can bring misfortune upon his army:

1 By commanding the army to advance or retreat, being ignorant of the fact that they cannot obey. This is called choking the army.

2 By participating in all military affairs when they are not fully aware of the military's status and situations. This causes confusion in the soldier's minds.

3 By trying to take on the job of controlling the military when they do not know the military principle of adaptation to circumstances. This causes the troops to doubt, question, and lose confidence.

When the army is confused and doubtful the other feudal lords will be rebellious, and thus our army will be lost and the enemy will be victorious."

[Translation]

In history, it was always ill-fated when the king and the general's relationship was shaky and they weren't in harmony before going into war. One of the actions the king should not interfere with is the decision to advance or retreat because the circumstances and situation can only be known by the general. The king should not interfere with military internal affairs because this brings disorder to the chain of command of the whole army. Lastly, the king should not interfere with the scheme or a plot (權謀術數) because it hurts the general's ability to adapt to the circumstances (臨機應變). These are the acts that will hand over victory to the enemy.

As was explained in the Understanding the Team section, this quote helps illustrate why the parents should not get too involved in coaching, analyzing, and/or giving strategy if they don't have a solid understanding of tennis. Ordering their players when to attack and defend, giving instructions to the player, and giving strategy over the coach's strategy are very common mistakes that parents make. The actual problem is that the parents don't know that they are making a mistake and they are doing more harm than good by trying too hard to help the player. No matter how many books or manuals a person reads and studies, it does not give them the combat experience and intuition that most coaches and players gain through experience. Some things are better left unsaid and trusting the player to do their job will definitely give them more confidence, the ability to adapt to situations, and the courage to be creative or open minded on the court.

In history, great leaders and kings have escorted their generals from the palace as they went into the battlefield and said, "I will take care of all the matters inside the palace, please take care of the matters outside of the palace," and no instructions were given. "Good luck and believe in yourself," is all that is needed to be said.

e) Five ways to victory

> *"Thus, victory can be realized by these five essentials:*
>
> *1 He who knows when to fight and when not to fight will win.*
>
> *2 He who knows how to use a large number of troops and small number of troops will win.*
>
> *3 If the general and the troops at all ranks are single minded will win.*
>
> *4 He who is prepared waiting for an enemy that is unprepared will win.*
>
> *5 If the general is competent and the king does not try to control they will win.*
>
> *These are the five essentials to realize victory."*

[Translation]

The keys to victory can be simple. Precise judgment, flexibility of tactics, united mindset, preparation, and exemption from political interference. It seems very obvious, but truth exists in the center of the ordinary. People of higher ranks and the lower ranks must be strongly united in order to keep the enemy from invading their trust. It does not matter how many weapons or how skilled the player is if the player does not feel like there's anyone on their side psychologically. Even though they might not feel like it, often the parents or coaches want the player to win just for their own pride and benefits. The player needs to feel that the parents and the coach are behind the player supporting them. That means when the player misjudges situations or makes unforced errors, the team should have empathy for them and try to solve the problem, not try to blame them for every mistake they make. It's easy for parents and coaches to feel like they are supporting them, but it's important to know exactly what the player is actually feeling.

Also, looking at the quote 上下同欲者勝 in the original book, it means that non-intervention from the king is the motivation and the driving force behind a victory. The parents should try not to interfere and cause confusion even if they were to repeat what the coach said to the player, since the player might take things differently if it is worded differently or said by the parents. Remember that interfering and showing interest are two different acts.

Not only is it important for parents to be patient; it is very important for the players to be able to communicate with their coach and parents. By being able to say what's on their mind, they will be able to open up to the parents and their coach, building trust in the relationship. For the parents and coaches, they'll be able to understand better about their player to be able to speak to them in the right tone.

f) If you know the enemy and know yourself, you need not fear the result of a hundred battles

> "Hence the saying: If you know the enemy and know yourself, you need not fear the result of a hundred battles. If you know yourself but not the enemy, for every victory gained you will also suffer defeat. If you know neither the enemy nor yourself, you will put yourself in danger of defeat in every battle."

[Translation]

Gaining precise knowledge about the opponent is imperative to gain victory. Trusting only their abilities, misinterpreting the knowledge to one's own advantage, or being elated from a recent victory will make the player ignorant of their opponents, which will ruin the match. Having confidence is different from being conceited and arrogant. Sun Tzu is explaining that no matter what the situation, being able to clearly analyze oneself and the opponent is key to victory. His mention of knowing both sides can mean that, more often than not, it is true that a battle is fought with shallow views of the enemy and oneself.

Before knowing the opponent, players need to know themselves. This is one of the reasons why top players seem so stubborn and do not like to change to new rackets, strings, and other equipment very often. It is important to be able to adapt to new situations, but changing a racket changes their feel, control, and the effects of the shot, therefore making it necessary to work on their shots to be able to know exactly what is possible and what is not possible with the equipment. Adding another variable to a match, not knowing themselves, and not having enough time with the new equipment to know the full capability makes it very difficult to have confidence in themselves in a match. Not every player is as sensitive to equipment changes, and coaches and parents probably have taught the player the "it's the magician, not the wand" mentality, but as the competition gets stiff, finding an edge over an opponent is critical, and it is important for the player to use equipment that is fit for them.

Another reason why the players need to know themselves is because the type of strategy they will employ is closely related to how good of a game they have. The players need to know how good of a game they have. No matter how good your strategies or theories might be, if you don't have the technical aspect of your game down, it is not possible to employ any type of strategy. Strategy is limited by the quality of the player's game. This is why it is so important to keep developing the player's game to be able to compete at the top level. The coach should be able to teach the players different types of shots according to different situations (Chapter 5 – Form of Power). This is why learning proper technique and adding new shots is so important at every stage of a tennis player's career. It is to be able to add their own creative mind to play different strategies and tactics on the court according to different situations and the type of opponent they are playing. Not only is it important to learn at every stage of the career, but it is crucial to learn to play properly from the beginning to prevent a player from hitting a potential wall and plateauing in the middle of their career. A player might not be hindered by their athleticism or mental capacity, but because of their actual skill or ability to hit shots due to the bad habits formed over the years.

Knowing oneself is not as easy as it seems. A player expects a shot, easy shot, nearly impossible shot, or any shot in fact, to work every time because the brain is imagining that the shot is going to be successful. The more perfectionist a player is, the clearer the images of a shot being successful because they believe and expect themselves to succeed. Figuring out and analyzing oneself in terms of what is possible and what is not without imaginative positives are the keys to improvement. Analyzing oneself takes time, and frequent failure is simply a part of finding a way something needs to be done. What closes the gap between imagination and reality on the court is practice. Watching a top pro on TV can help generate the images in the player's, brain but actually being able to make a shot in reality is the result of time spent on practicing a particular shot. Knowing oneself and self-belief occurs when a player knows "how" it is done and has experienced success previously and has the confidence to do "it" again. Self-belief does not come to oneself if they haven't experienced success yet. Striving to successfully hit a tough shot and trying to perfect it comes from perseverance and discipline.

IV.

DISPOSITION OF THE MILITARY (形) – PLAYERS' TENDENCIES, STYLE OF PLAY, AND BASE POWER

In the book The Art of War, this chapter is about the physical disposition of the military. In other words, it's the physical form of offense and defense. It is the contrasting notion to the next chapter Form of Power (勢), but the two notions complement each other. Since form of power (勢) or strategical flexibility is formed from the basis of the disposition (形) of the military and the disposition (形) of the military is defined by the form of power (勢), it cannot be said which is more important than the other.

Physical disposition will be translated into the physical disposition of the player. When people discuss a player's style, they often refer to them as an offensive player or a defensive player. From there, it can be broken down into aggressive baseliner, counter-puncher, pusher, all-around player, and so on. Physical disposition of a player can be very closely related to the form of attack/power the player prefers, which is the tactics, strategy, and the mental part of their game. The physical disposition of the player is the foundation of the form of attack/power they will be using to dominate their opponents. In other words, the offensive or defensive tendencies and the style the player plays is very closely related to the shot selection and strategies that they use to win a match.

a) Neutralize your enemy

> *"The good fighters in the past have prevented the enemy from victory, and have waited for the opportunity to defeat the enemy. Securing ourselves against defeat lies in our own hands and the opportunity of defeating the enemy is provided by the enemy himself.*
>
> *Thus the good fighter is able to secure himself against defeat, but cannot make victory certain by forcing the enemy to defeat. Hence victory can be known ahead of time but victory cannot be made to happen.*
>
> *Security against defeat implies defensive tactics; ability to defeat the enemy means taking the offensive. Standing on the defensive indicates insufficient strength; offensive, a superabundance of strength.*
>
> *The general who is skilled in defense hides in the most secret recesses of the earth; he who is skilled in attack flashes forth from the topmost heights of heaven. Thus we can protect ourselves whilst earning a complete victory."*

[Translation]

The emphasis in this section is to prevent the enemy from achieving victory. No one can guarantee victory in war, but one must prevent the enemy from achieving victory. The quote, *"securing ourselves against defeat lies in our own hands..."* seems defensive, but the phrase has to be understood accurately. Neutralizing and defending is just as important as attacking. This section is not about being defensive; it is about waiting for the right opportunity to attack without unforced errors. While waiting for the right time to attack, it is crucial not to show (unintentionally) any vulnerabilities to the enemy for them to be able to go on the offensive. Sun Tzu's disposition of the army was an undefeatable (不敗) army. It was not to win at all cost (必勝). No matter how strong and fierce the army, the outcome will be uncertain when they are matched up against the enemy and the circumstances and situations change during the battle. This is why it was more important to secure themselves from defeat rather than pulverize everything in their path.

Every time a shot is struck in tennis, the shot has to be offensive and defensive at the same time. Although the physical disposition of a player at the top level looks very offensive, their mental disposition can actually be slightly defensive. Defensive, meaning the pro players do not take chances of missing a shot very often (unforced errors) or giving the opponent a chance to attack. Although pros look like they are very offensive, surprisingly, pro players do not like taking risks and rely heavily on their intuition and strategies to defeat their opponents. This can mean that the player is mentally defensive, but the actual shots are offensive. Playing offensive tennis is often thought of as the best way to play, but playing smart is the best way to play. Not only does playing slightly defensive (mentally conservative to minimize unforced errors) give the opponent a chance to miss or misplay a point, but it gives the player an idea of how the opponent attacks and a feel for the opponent. In other words, it gives the player an opportunity to look for openings to attack. Pro players look offensive because they've practiced thousands and thousands of times playing offensively and are consistent playing offensively just as much as playing defensively (although mentally they might not always be comfortable with defending). Remember, the chances of them playing offensive tennis are played at the highest percentage allowed for them that day. The amazing and high risk shots hit at the highest level in tennis are the result of their calculations for the highest possibility of winning that point. For example, if a pro player is stretched out wide on the forehand side and has a very low chance of winning the point if the shot is hit down the middle of the court, crosscourt, or a lob, then the player will take their chance to win the point by hitting a winner down the line if their ability allows it because hitting a mediocre shot down the middle will certainly give the opponent a clear chance to win the point. In juniors and amateur tennis, it would be best to hit the wide forehand defensively and have their opponent hit another shot since the chances of hitting a perfect shot for a winner is fairly low and the probability of them hitting an amazing shot down the line is even lower. This is the reason why sometimes an up-and-coming junior player can beat a decent pro player. Most junior players tend to go for shots that are high risk and low percentage even on shots that do not require risk taking, and on a good day, they might be hitting amazing shots all throughout the match, but this strategy is basically relying on luck. Winning a tournament requires much more mental and physical skill than winning just one match.

So the question is why do coaches emphasize offensive disposition so much when developing a player? It is to have them get used to attacking so much that they don't feel like they are being that offensive because they've played that way for so long. As it is with temporal illusions in the field of time perception, a person may perceive time as slowing down or stopping when a certain motion or an act is repeated for a long duration of time. For example, a beginning tennis player can describe the ball leaving the strings on their racket as instant, but for a pro, it can be described that the ball stays on the strings for a very long time to be able to control the ball the way they would like. Playing offensive tennis can feel very hectic and out of control at their developmental stage, but if done right, as time goes by, the time a ball comes off the opponent's racket to their side will seem to get rather long and the player will be able to stay composed. This should enable the player to shift their actual disposition from offensive plays and defensive plays freely from one another depending on the situation. In addition, being offensive and playing offensive style of tennis at a young age helps the player to attack without fear at the right moment when they need to attack. When the players play too defensively at a young age, they will not be able to attack when the opportunity arises. The window of opportunity to attack during a point gets smaller as the level gets higher and it will be difficult for a player that's played defensive all their life to be able to attack with such a low probability of making the shot in their mind.

The quote *"...the opportunity of defeating the enemy is provided by the enemy himself..."* not only has to do with an opponent actually hitting an easy ball to the player, but it can also be thought of as giving an opportunity to break their service game. Most pros, especially on the men's side, have capable serves to hold their serve. Although return of serves are getting better in modern tennis, the serve is still an offensive weapon because the point has to be started with a serve. Clearly being on the offensive position, it is up to the server to be able to keep a high percentage of first serves in, first serve points won, and dictating with the shot after the return. Feeling the nerves and mentally breaking down happens internally and the player must fight the tension and stay calm. There are times when service breaks happen by the returner playing a flawless game, but more times than not, the service break is given by the server, not the returner forcing the break of serve within that game.

Finally, physical disposition of the player can be described as how the player chooses to neutralize their opponents. This physical disposition can be offensive or defensive, but whichever way a pro decides to neutralize the opponent has more to do with their ability, strength, and mental tendencies, and not their conscious decisions. By asking a player with a defensive disposition to attack all out by hitting aggressive and big shots, the player will only lose confidence. Same goes for players that have offensive dispositions, by asking them to play a defensive "get every ball back" mentality, they might feel edgy and make poor shot selections, thus losing confidence in their ability to attack. For an aggressive player, the best defense might be offensive tennis and for a defensive player, their best offense might be defense. Knowing your player's mentality and fully understanding them is important to be able to teach and coach them based on their specific needs.

b) "Way to fight out there" is not a compliment

> *"When predicting victory in war, using the means of the common herd cannot be known as the best stratagem. When a war is fought and won and the whole Empire says, "Good fight!" it is not a victory well done. Thus, one does not put a lot of effort in lifting the autumn feathers; does not use their keen sights to see the sun and the moon; and does not need to listen closely to the noise of thunder. What ancients called a clever fighter is one who not only wins, but excels in winning with ease. Hence his victories bring him neither reputation for wisdom nor credit for courage but wins battles by making no mistakes. Making no mistakes means to take measures to establish certainty of victory, by conquering an enemy that is already defeated. Hence the skillful fighter puts himself into the grounds of which makes defeat impossible, and does not miss the moment for defeating the enemy. Thus it is that in war the victorious strategist only seeks battle after the victory has been won, whereas he who is destined to defeat first fights and afterwards looks for victory. The consummate leader cultivates the moral law, and strictly adheres to method and discipline; thus it is in his power to control success."*

[Translation]

The first half of this passage indicates that the ones who are proficient at warfare not only achieve victory but achieve it handily. If the whole empire knows how you have fought and talks about the great battle, then it also means that you have exposed too much to everyone regarding how you fight. Sometimes a tennis match can look great when two players are playing fast-paced aggressive tennis with no one backing down or making it look like an intense battle, but then we often see the winner of an amazing match lose really easily in the next round. The player that won that intense battle could have been physically tired or have been satisfied with the last win, but losing the subsequent match might be because the opponent utilized their weaknesses better and avoided going up against their strengths. Two players playing into each other's strengths might be fun to watch, but it can also mean that they don't have any other styles or strategies that they can use to dictate their opponents.

The second half of the passage explains that winning doesn't have to be all dazzling and flamboyant. Making it look easy without any mistakes is what makes the great fighters so deadly, while not making a mistake looking for the opportunity to attack and seizing the moment when the opponent is vulnerable. "No mistakes" in the verse *"...Hence his victories bring him neither reputation for wisdom nor credit for courage but wins battles by making no mistakes..."* does not only mean that they don't miss while playing a match. It can mean both unforced errors and the judgment to attack or defend. Knowing which shot they can attack and which shot to defend is crucial in tennis. Knowing and being able to cover the court where the opponent will attack and attacking the opponent as soon as they show an opening is how some of the best players play tennis.

c) The road to complete victory

> "In respect of military method, we have, firstly, Measurement (度 – measurement of distance between enemy and our forces), secondly, Estimation of movement (量 – mobilization power), thirdly, Estimation of Numbers (數 – number of troops), fourthly, Balance of power (稱 – weighing the power between enemy and our forces), fifthly, Victory (勝 – probability of victory). The existence of Earth constitutes Measurement, Measurement constitutes Estimation of Movement, Estimation of Movement constitutes Estimation of Numbers, Estimation of Numbers helps constitutes Balance of Power, and thus balancing act brings us to victory.
>
> A victorious army opposed to a routed one, is as a pound's weight placed in the scale against a single grain. The onrush of a conquering force is like the bursting of pent-up waters into a chasm of a thousand fathoms deep. This is the Disposition of the Military (形)."

[Translation]

The military method can be translated into the following for tennis:

Earth – the tennis court

1) Measurement – positioning of the opponent and oneself and the space between the target and oneself
2) Estimation of movement – The ability to move and the fitness level of the player (量 – at that time was used to measure the weight of crops)

3) Estimation of numbers – Number of weapons a player possesses
4) Balance of power – comparing the opponent's strengths and weaknesses to oneself
5) Victory – The result of the calculations

Measurement can relate to the positioning of the opponent and oneself and the space between the target and oneself. When playing a point, the player will have to measure where they are standing, where the opponent is standing, a shot's target has to be set according to the opponent's position, then the measurement of the player and the distance between the target has to be measured to be able to calculate how much spin or power has to be used to place the ball.

Estimation of movement can relate to the ability to move to the ball and the fitness level of the player. The player must be able to move to the ball fast enough to set up (dynamic and stationary setup) properly to hit an effective shot, and the fitness level will allow the player to move fast consistently on the court.

Estimation of numbers can relate to the number of weapons a player possesses. Just like different units require different type of troops, weapon is not just a stroke, serve, forehand, or a backhand, but a certain shot in a given situation. For example, a player can have a very good backhand down the line that is low and fast while on the run or a forehand shot that can hit a high and slow ball without any pace in the middle of the court for a winner. There can be many weapons within a stroke and can be distinguished by breaking the stroke into situational shots.

Balance of power can relate to measuring the opponent's weapons against the player themselves, which then leads to winning the point, victory. Measuring the opponent's weapons against the player themselves means how well a player can defend or counterattack the balls that the opponent hit using their strengths to attack.

Sun Tzu focuses on securing oneself from defeat and looking for the opportunity to attack in this chapter and the last verse *"… The onrush of a conquering force is like the bursting of pent-up waters into a chasm of a thousand fathoms deep. This is the Disposition of the Military (形),"* sums up the chapter pretty nicely. The pent-up water is calm, and it's placed there strategically and it is waiting to be released to sweep up everything in its path. While waiting for an opportunity to attack, the player must stay calm without unforced errors; then when the opportunity arises, they should attack swiftly, powerfully, and concentrated into their opening, which can't be stopped like the water bursting into the chasm.

V.

FORM OF POWER (勢)
– STRATEGICAL FLEXIBILITY
AND SHOT SELECTION

Form of power (勢) in the book The Art of War covers the potential elements and forms that can be changed by the army while in battle. The method of controlling the enemy's physical disposition with strategical flexibility is understood as form of power (勢). Hiding true self (藏形), showing of untrue self (示形), exposing the enemy (形人) are also forms of power. It's a form of killer instinct in which the player changes their form of attack to make the opponent miserable. Swift decisions, flexibility in battle, thorough training with weapons, and digging into the enemy's weakness are emphasized in this chapter.

If physical disposition of the player helps them wait and open up opportunities to attack, form of power is the actual ability to attack and the ability to change their form of attack. Hitting aggressive and powerful shots is only one way of playing. The best part about being able to hit big is not the ability itself to hit big, but it is the potential ability to add another form of deception to attack the opponent, which can open up opportunities to use other touch shots or angle shots more effectively. When playing a match, practical use of the player's abilities and the ability to change according to the environment and situation is important.

Although an offensive (physically powerful) game is highly rated by most, it is not possible with physically weaker players. Strategical flexibility of a defensive player (limited by their physical strength) is often overlooked by most people and is very difficult to gauge how capable they are. Most feel-based and defensive players attack their opponents with their own form of power and hide their true weapons until the probability of winning the point with their weapon is very high.

It is important to know that deception and child's play (playing around with a shot) are two different forms of play. The player has to experience what works and what doesn't by exploring and learning new shots and actually using them in the match to see how well they have to hit it and experience when to use the shot. This is why winning is not always the key to developing. In order for the player to explore what they are capable of, they need to be able to try and fail as much as succeed in winning. Losing is not always losing; not being able to analyze why the loss happened is a true loss.

a) Know-hows of executing the strategies

> *"The control of a large force is the same principle as the control of a few men: it is merely a question of dividing (分數) up their numbers. Fighting with a large army under your command is nowise different from fighting with a small one: it is merely a question of instituting signs and signals (形名). To ensure that your whole host may withstand the brunt of the enemy's attack and remain unshaken – this is effected by direct and indirect maneuvers (奇正). That the impact of your army may be like a grindstone dashed against an egg – this is effected by the science of weak points and strong (虛實)."*

[Translation]

This passage explains the ways to execute the strategies. It can be understood as the basis of flexibility in tactics and the mind. The four know-hows are translated into tennis as:

1. Dividing (分數) – Clearly dividing and knowing when to use what shot
2. Signs and signals (形名) – Reading the opponent's movements and their court positioning
3. Direct and indirect maneuvers (奇正) – Using head-on tactics and surprise/unexpected tactics
4. Weaknesses and strengths (虛實) – Attacking the opponent's weakness with the player's strength

In order for the player to be able to use direct and indirect maneuvers and weaknesses and strengths, the dividing of when to attack and when to use what shot has to be clear. In order for the division of shot selection to be clear, the signs and signals from the opponent have to be read by the player.

The player must be able to differentiate their own shots from offensive, counter, neutral, defensive shots to be able to decide on what shot they will use. Knowing when to use what shot is known by the opponent's movements and their court positioning. According to the opponent's movement and their court positioning, the player should be able to tell what type of shot the opponent will be hitting and can decide to use what type of attack to make on the next shot. When deciding on what type of shot they will use to attack, they need to decide on where to attack, to their strengths or to their weaknesses.

Flexibility in the mind and the mental concentration needed to do this comes from training and experience in matches. The parents getting involved in every match emotionally will hinder the player's decisions in a match because they will be afraid of making mistakes and choosing the wrong shots. On the other hand, the tactician or the coach is only watching the player's moves emotionlessly to be able to teach the players whether it was the right shot or tactic to use after the match is complete. Also the coach can judge if the player was able to execute the shots and tactics practiced in training and if the player couldn't execute; the coach can clearly differentiate if the tactics and shots were unable to be used because of the player's ability or if the opponent was not allowing the player to be able to use those tactics. Many parents complain that their player wasn't able to play like in practice. It is not only a matter of whether they can or not, but whether the opponent lets them or not. The situation in a match might not have allowed the player to be able to play a certain style or hit a certain type of shots. There's a lot more to shot selection than hitting the ball as hard as possible to be aggressive.

The keywords in the book *The Art of War* can be narrowed down to direct and indirect maneuvers and strengths and weaknesses. Strengths and weaknesses are not simply the exposed strengths and weaknesses of a player. The ability to hide their weaknesses and also being able to make the opponent think a weakness is a strength is all in the meaning of strengths and weaknesses.

b) Tactics that paralyze the senses

> *"In all fighting, the direct method may be used to face battles, but indirect methods will be needed in order to secure victory. Indirect tactics, efficiently applied, are inexhaustible as Heaven and Earth, unending as the flow of rivers and streams; like the sun and moon, they end but to begin anew; like the four seasons, they pass away to return once more. There are not more than five musical notes, yet the combinations of these five give rise to more melodies than can ever be heard. There are not more than five primary colors (blue, yellow, red, white, and black), yet in combination they produce more hues than can ever been seen. There are not more than five cardinal tastes (sour, acrid, salt, sweet, bitter), yet combinations of them yield more flavors than can ever be tasted. In battle, there are not more than two methods of attack – the direct and the indirect; yet these two in combination give rise to an endless series of maneuvers. The direct and the indirect lead on to each other in turn. It is like moving in a circle – you never come to an end. Who can exhaust the possibilities of their combination?"*

[Translation]

Even for tennis, tactics on a large scale can be divided into two forms, direct and indirect methods. Direct being head-on and standard tactics and indirect being deceptive and surprise tactics. A player that is capable is not only a player that can strike the ball clean, but a player that can change the form of their attack infinitely. In order for deceptive and surprise attacks to work effectively, their ability to fight the opponent head-on has to be trustworthy. Being able to play against the opponent head-on means that the player's rally balls and average shots must be effective and be able to pressure the opponent. Pressuring the opponent with their rally ball is not enough to secure victory at the top level, so the method of deception and surprise attacks must be used. Hitting the ball on the rise on a fast-paced ball, coming in to the net when the opponent is on the run and did not expect the player to come in, backing up behind the baseline and making it look like they are defending but attacking with a fast-paced lower shot, making it look like coming in to the net on a slice but hitting a drop-shot to fool the opponent, and serving and volleying when the opponent least expects it are some surprise attacks that a player can use. Another type of direct and indirect methods are when a player receives a short ball to attack, it can be hit to an opponent's weakness most of the time and at a crucial time, the player can attack to their strengths when they least expect it to make them unprepared. The combination can be infinite and the decisions are made by the player as they play the match.

When the player is playing a match, they must be solid but be able to adapt to circumstances and attack the opponent's weaknesses; this is the basis of the strategy. In lower form of tennis, being solid (consistent) is the most difficult but the most effective strategy. Worrying about the opponent's strengths and weaknesses is less crucial to winning because the ability and the shots to attack their weaknesses might be lacking. As the competition gets stronger, it is crucial to be able to change forms of attack and hide their own weaknesses, meaning the foundation and technique gets important once again after the phase of learning the tactics is completed.

c) Importance of momentum and quality of shot selection

> *"The onset (勢) of troops is like the rush of a torrent which will even roll stones along in its course. The quality(swift and precise) of decision (節) is like the well-timed swoop of a falcon which enables it to strike and destroy its victim. Therefore the good fighter will be intense in his onset, and prompt in his decision. Energy (勢) may be likened to the bending of a crossbow; decision (節), to the releasing of a trigger."*

[Translation]

Momentum should be rough and intense and the decisions should be short and swift. The decision to attack should be made swiftly and precisely once the player sees an opportunity to attack. Once the decision is made to attack, the attack should have enough momentum and force like water violently going down through a river, sweeping everything in its path.

d) Baiting and counter-attacking

> *"Amid the turmoil and tumult of battle, there may be seeming disorder and yet no real disorder at all; amid confusion and chaos, our forces and the enemy must not be mixed and if the battle array is round, it will prevent from total defeat. Simulated disorder postulates perfect discipline, simulated fear postulates courage; simulated weakness postulates strength. Hiding order beneath the cloak of disorder is simply a question of subdivision (分數); concealing courage under a show of timidity presupposes a fund of latent energy (勢); masking strength with weakness is to be effected by strategical dispositions (形). Thus one who is skillful at keeping the enemy on the move maintains deceitful appearances, according to which the enemy will act. He sacrifices something, that the enemy may snatch at it. By holding out baits, he keeps him on the march; then with a body of picked men he lies in wait for him."*

[Translation]

From this passage and to the end of the chapter, it sets up the use of Chapter 6: Weaknesses and Strengths. The passage starts off by saying that one should not play into the opponent's game and have to have a purpose to each action, even when the player looks like they are leaving an opening while they are attacking, it is still based on the player's calculations to bait the opponent. While on the offensive, it is easy to lose purpose of why and how you're attacking the enemy, thus giving the opponent a chance to attack back. By simulating or faking a weakness, you can control the opponent at your will by anticipating the attack of the opponent to set up a counterattack.

Showing a weakness on purpose takes discipline, guts, and the ability to counterattack. The term counter-puncher in high level tennis is used to describe a very defensive player. Although that does make sense, being able to counter-punch is very important in tennis even for aggressive players. Picking the right shots to attack by luring an opponent is a great strategy. For example, turning around on a ball that should clearly be hit with a backhand to hit an inside out or an inside in forehand leaves lots of room for the opponent to be able to attack the open court. That also means that the player that turned around can read their opponent's next shot because the massive open court will make it seem foolish to not attack the open court. Assuming the inside out or inside in was hit effectively, the opponent has no choice but to hit to the open court, thus giving the player the option to attack or counterattack on the next shot. But all this can only be possible if the player is able to quickly decide to turn around to hit a forehand, hit the inside in or inside out effectively, be fast enough to cover the court, and have the confidence and the ability to attack or counterattack on the next shot. Another example is when a short ball is hit purposely, making it just good enough to prevent the opponent from hitting an effective approach shot but bringing the opponent in to the net to be able to hit a passing shot or a lob. There are infinite numbers of strategical plays that can be used according to the situation and the flow of the match. By using direct and indirect attacks and using strengths and weaknesses to a player's advantage, the opponent can be controlled to move at the player's will. Purposely hitting soft and getting the ball back down the middle can also be a strategy when the opponent is only relying on their ability to hit big. Big hitters have a high chance of being arrogant and they are usually very proud of their ability to hit big; then the player can capitalize on their strength and turn it into a weakness. Over-hitting occurs very often in tennis because being defensive is berated by everyone. By using that against the opponent, it can be a very useful tool. Hitting big shots over and over can build pressure on an opponent and if the defending player has the confidence to get everything back, then this tactic can be used to break down an opponent. The opponent is basically breaking down internally, not really knowing what they are doing wrong. Players that are very offensive like to keep the points short and are not concerned by an opponent attacking them. What they do not like is persistence and tenacious opponents that don't seem to go away. Using defensive measures to break down an opponent is then the ultimate offense. Once the opponent changes their offensive nature to become overly aggressive or passive, then the defending player can take charge and go on the offensive to harass the opponent. This method is also very useful to deploy on a very defensive opponent. By giving them a ball they can attack, it will then force the opponent to be in an attacking position, which then leaves room to counterattack.

Although indirect methods or deception are a huge part of strategy in tennis, there are times when deception does not work. When deception does not work, it can mean a couple things. 1) The opponent is more experienced or at a higher level than the player, thus the deceptive tactics are being read. 2) The player did not use head-on tactics enough before using deceptive tactics to fool the opponent. 3) The quality of the shots hit to deceive or trick the opponent were not high enough (child's play). The player must analyze what is happening during the match by using this reasoning. When the opponent is at a higher level than the player, then it is better to attack them head-on or hit bigger rally balls to prevent the opponent from reading the player's moves and to prevent the opponent from using deceptive tactics. By raising the level of the player, the player is taking risks of missing rally balls by attacking them constantly, but it might be the best chance to beat the higher level opponent. The third reason a deceptive tactic might not be effective is because the shots being hit are a joke to the opponent. For example, acting like the player is going to hit a big shot but changing the shot in the middle of the shot to hit a drop shot can be a deceptive play, but to make the shot effective, the quality of the drop shot is still very important. Differentiating what can be done and what can't be done can define how mature the player is during a match, but just because they missed or hit a drop shot does not mean that it was not the correct shot to hit. By blaming the player for missing a drop shot, it can hinder their creativity on the court. If the player is ready to add drop shot to their game, working on the drop shot to make the tactic effective is key.

e) Momentum is fed by shot selection

> *"The clever combatant looks to the effect of combined energy (勢), and does not require too much from individuals. Hence his ability to pick out the right men and utilize combined energy. When he utilizes combined energy, his fighting men become as it were like unto rolling logs or stones. For it is the nature of a log or stone to remain motionless on level ground, and move when on a slope; if four-cornered, to come to a standstill, but if round-shaped, to go rolling down. Thus the energy developed by the general is as the momentum of a round stone rolled down a mountain thousands of feet in height. So much on the subject of energy."*

[Translation]

Picking the right men can help utilize the momentum. Picking the right men to do a specific job in the battlefield is critical. A spearman is effective at handling cavalry, cavalry is strong against a swordsman, and swordsmen are effective at handling spearmen at close range. By choosing the right men and controlling them at will, the general is able to create momentum for the army. Just because the general believes in the strength of their cavalry, it does not mean he should use his cavalry against the enemy spearmen. Since a great general knows the advantages and disadvantages of specific men fighting different type of units, the general is able to create momentum by choosing the right men to keep them advantageous in a fight.

Having a limited amount of shots to work with, but the ability to pick out the right shots in each situation to be advantageous, is much more important than having an array of weapons and using them individually without any purpose. Efficient shot selection can keep a player's momentum by constantly making the opponent feel like the player is attacking them. Thus, breaking them down and rolling through their opponents. Again, this can only be done with an array of shots in the player's arsenal. A player that has a lot of weapons has the potential to be a great competitor, but they need to be taught to limit themselves to a few of their best options because they have so many weapons to work with and they believe in their abilities too much, which makes them take unnecessary risks. Although it is important to learn shot selection no matter what type of player they are, it is significantly more important for a player with various weapons to learn how to use their weapons at the right time. A player that is technically sound might not need fundamental or technical training, but may need tactical and mental training. By teaching the player that has many weapons to select the correct shots, they can excel much faster than focusing on the basics and fundamentals. While teaching the player that has many weapons, the player can feel suffocated because of the fact that they are limiting possibilities, but the players must be wise and control themselves and listen to the coaches, and the coaches have to be wise to help the player understand what would happen based on their reckless shot selections.

Another example of using the *"combined energy and not requiring too much from individual"* means that they should use all of their shots and not just rely on one weapon that a player has. When playing a match, a stroke can break down or it can even feel bad before starting the match. For a player that has to play a match, it is important to think about how they will cover up the weakness by using other strokes and shots. For example, if a player's first serve is not feeling up to par with other weapons that the player has and they are unable to solve the problem during the match, then the player should try to keep the first serve percentage high and focus on attacking or counterattacking the next shot. Knowing that the serve is going to get attacked, the player should stay alert and move quickly to hit the next shot effectively to be able to dictate the opponent rather than focusing too much on trying to fix the shot completely during a match.

f) Zoning in tennis

Zoning in tennis happens when the thoughts of a player can be performed physically. The physical disposition and the flexibility in the mind working in perfect harmony. Therefore it does not feel like the player is thinking and every movement feels like a flow of instinctive movements rather than artificial. When a player is zoning, the strengths and weaknesses of an opponent can be clearly seen as they do not have to focus on themselves. The mind can trigger the zoning, but the actual limitations of keeping it is more in the physical ability to keep it. In a perfect scenario, the mind can think of infinite ways to win a point, but realistically, more often than not, actually being able to hit the shots is limited by the player's physical abilities. Players unknowingly change their technique to adapt to their opponents or situations, which only the most sensitive coaches can see. Therefore, it is almost impossible to keep the same technique or feel for longer than two weeks at a time. When the player is able to keep it more than two weeks, then it is not zoning, but it is their acquired ability to sustain that level of play.

So when a player is zoning, it is not their true level, but if the greatness continues, then it can be timidly concluded that the zoning was in fact their ability. So when a player is still developing and adding new dimensions to their game, they can zone in and out at times, but to sustain that level is a lot more difficult. To be able to sustain the highest level, self-discipline, proper training, and experience all have to be fulfilled.

VI.

WEAKNESSES AND STRENGTHS (虛實)

Weaknesses can be strengths and strengths can be weaknesses. This chapter is about applying them appropriately in strategy. It's the most fundamental and practical of all chapters. The idea is to come out of the passive state of analyzing and realizing the enemy's weakness and capitalizing on the enemy's weaknesses to move your opponent at your will. The previous chapter was about capitalizing on an opportunity to attack by using various direct and indirect tactics. The difference in this chapter is the changes in tactics based on the weaknesses of an opponent or to use the player's Form of Power into the opponent's weaknesses. Weaknesses and strengths can also be translated into dispersion and assembly, which means to disperse the enemy's strengths by attacking the opponent's strengths and further exposing their weaknesses by exploiting the opponent's strategy to defend their weaknesses. It can also be used to counter an opponent by purposely luring an opponent to attack or by knowing the player's own weaknesses to lure an opponent to set up a certain shot. At every level from the intermediates to the pros, the players are most likely playing a match against someone on a similar level, so it might not be easy to see the opponent's distinct strengths and weaknesses during a match. In the lower levels of tennis, weaknesses and strengths are more pronounced and are easy to spot or pick on, such as a weaker backhand than the forehand. In the higher level of tennis, strengths and weaknesses are not only defined by the quality of the shot, but it also has to do with being comfortable or uncomfortable in certain situations. For example, a player can be forced to a situation where he or she might have to attack a high and heavy ball and puts it away for a winner. Although the player might have executed flawlessly, in actuality the player might have executed as best as they can to hide the fact that they don't like to hit the highball so the opponent won't do it again. Knowing that the opponent is comfortable or not can be tricky and is not easily seen just by technical standards, but it must be felt by the player and the coach intuitively by taking the opponent's physical and mental dispositions and their patterns of play into account. The depth of which a player has to use the weaknesses into strengths and strengths to weaknesses is endless, but it is so subtle at the top level that unless you're an expert in reading player's moves, it is very difficult to understand. Although this is the most fundamental and practical chapter, ignoring the physical dispositions and the form of power chapter and working only on exploiting weaknesses won't work in the higher levels since the opponents' weaknesses are not very obvious and the player must have the ability and the skills to exploit the opponent's weaknesses.

a) Get there before the opponent (opponent's shots)

> "Whoever is first in the field and awaits the coming of the enemy, will be fresh for the fight; whoever is second in the field and has to hasten to battle will arrive exhausted. Therefore the clever combatant lures the enemy to them and is not dragged into a fight. He can cause the enemy to approach by his own will because it seems as it is advantageous for the enemy, or, he can make it impossible for the enemy to draw near because it seems as though it is damaging for the enemy. If the enemy is taking his ease, he can harass him; if well supplied with food, he can starve him out; if quietly encamped, he can force him to move. Appear at points which the enemy must hasten to defend; march swiftly to places where you are not expected."

[Translation]

In order to control the enemy, there are three rules to be followed: thorough preparation, psychological tactics, and appropriately applying intense and aggressive attacks to penetrate their weaknesses. One of the preparation phases in tennis is the anticipation and the movement to the ball. The player must be able to get to the ball early and set up to be able to have options to select different shots or hit the shot effectively. On the other hand, if the player is getting to the ball with just enough time to hit the ball, they will feel rushed and the percentage of hitting a high quality shot will be low and the options to hit various shots are very limited. When a player moves to strike the ball, they have to move like they are going to be where the ball will be struck faster than the ball does.

The psychological tactics in these phrases are to harass the opponent as much as they can by making them uneasy at every move they take. Making them do whatever is the opposite of their will, will get them confused and frustrated. As mentioned in Chapter 4, Section a, for an aggressive player, the best defense might be offensive tennis and for a defensive player, their best offense might be defense. Going deeper into the meaning of "a defensive player's best offense might be defense" means that the opponent will assume that they will defend. While thinking that the player will only defend, the opponent will relax and not be able to defend if the defensive player decides to attack.

The last quote can be translated perfectly as how and when a player should go in to the net to finish the point off with a volley. *"Appear at points which the enemy must hasten to defend; march swiftly to places where you are not expected,"* would be hitting a shot to have the opponent defend your shots so desperately that they cannot see you and the thought of the player coming in to the net did not even come across his or her mind. This is the principle of a modern approach shot in tennis. When a short ball that can be hit as an approach shot is given to a player, the opponent will realize that they hit short and will take measures to defend or counterattack. So the best time to go in to the net is when they do not expect the player to go in to the net. But one must remember that going in to the net with a low chance of winning the point just for the element of surprise is not the answer.

b) The rules of military march (court positioning) and defensive measures (anticipation)

> *"An army may march great distances without distress, if it marches through where the enemy is not present. You can be sure of succeeding in your attacks if you only attack places which are undefended. You can ensure the safety of your defense if you only hold positions that cannot be attacked (defend positions that will surely be attacked)."*

[Translation]

In warfare, a military march to a rendezvous point or a location causes considerable distress. The soldiers must battle with their inner selves of wanting to eat, drink, rest, and sleep while traveling long distances when supplies and rations are limited. As if that wasn't enough, if they suffer several surprise attacks while on the move, they will be exhausted even before they get to the battlefield. It is very important to avoid confrontations with the enemy to prevent wasting energy before getting to the rendezvous point. In tennis, this can relate to how a player should move to the ball by anticipating the opponent's moves and shots. It is much more physically demanding to sprint to the ball impulsively rather than anticipating the opponent's shots. The player needs to anticipate by analyzing and calculating the opponent's offensive, defensive, and movement capabilities. The quote *"You can ensure the safety of your defense if you only hold positions that cannot be attacked (defend positions that will surely be attacked),"* is the best way to describe how to counterpunch. By anticipating the methods and limitations of the opponent's attacks, the player can defend where it must be attacked, which gives the player enough chance to counterattack. This is one of the reasons why it's so difficult to go in to the net after hitting an approach shot. Hitting an approach shot on the first short ball a player receives in the middle of the court is too obvious at the pro level. Unless the opponent is having a tough time that day with hitting passing shots, it is best to go in to the net by sneaking in on a shot that is less predictable.

c) Unwritten laws of offense and defense

> *"Hence that general is skillful in attack whose opponent does not know what to defend; and he is skillful in defense whose opponent does not know what to attack. O divine art of subtlety and secrecy! Through you we learn to be in no form, through you inaudible; and hence we can hold the enemy's fate in our hands. You may advance and be absolutely irresistible, if you make for the enemy's weak points; you may retire and be safe from pursuit if your movements are more rapid than those of the enemy. If we wish to fight, the enemy can be forced to an engagement even though he be sheltered behind a high rampart and a deep ditch. All we need do is attack some other place that he will be obliged to relieve. If we do not wish to fight, we can prevent the enemy from engaging us even through the lines or our encampment be merely traced out on the ground. All we need do is to throw something odd and unaccountable in his way to steer him in the wrong way."*

[Translation]

Knowing the rules of defensive measures, the opponent must not know where and how the player will attack, and the opponent must not know what is being defended. The more subtle the differences between the player's offensive shots and defensive shots, the better. By making it difficult to distinguish your movements and shots, it will damage the opponent's ability to make swift judgments to decide on where to move and how to handle the next shot.

Usually, players are judged based on the average speed and the pace of the ball a player hits. If a very aggressive player can rally or play the point out with an average speed of 80 mph, but when they hit an attacking shot, they might still be able to hit it at 100 mph and still be safe from missing. The ability to rally and be consistent at 80 mph seems very difficult, but it might not be for an aggressive player because they have played aggressively their whole life and it doesn't feel like they are forcing the shot. If a player that has a 60 mph rally ball, without foot speed and defensive abilities, has to play a player that has an 80 mph rally ball, the player with the 60 mph rally ball has to play over their limit by playing at least 80 mph to be able to neutralize the player that can play at 80 mph consistently. This is why being able to hit big or super heavy consistently (player's disposition) is very important. It gives the player the options to drop the pace or rpm to stay even more consistent and play solid tennis or give them the advantage of being able to keep their shot speed or rpm even while they are on defense. It makes it difficult to distinguish between their offensive game and defensive game.

The quote, "... *Throw something odd and unaccountable in his way to steer him in the wrong way*" can be juking in tennis. Although it's not used very often, the player can make it look like they are defending or staying in a corner, then sprint to the other side to have the opponent hit to the side that they will run to.

d) Concentration and dispersing the concentration

> "By discovering the enemy's dispositions and remaining in no form ourselves, we can keep our forces concentrated, while the enemy's must be divided. We can form a single united body, while the enemy must split up into fractions. Hence there will be a whole pitted against separate parts of a whole, which means that we shall be many to the enemy's few. And if we are able thus to attack an inferior force with a superior one, our opponents will be in dire straits. The spot where we intend to fight must not be made known; for then the enemy will have to prepare against a possible attack at several different points; and his forces being thus distributed in many directions, the numbers we shall have to face at any given point will be proportionately few."

[Translation]

By knowing where and how the opponent will attack, the player can counterattack effectively. By keeping the opponent guessing where the player will attack, they can break up their defense by making the opponent cover all parts of the court rather than just a few positions. If the opponent has to defend too many parts of the court, then the opponent cannot focus on defending only their weakness. If they focus on guarding their weakness too much, then they open up the chance of being attacked to their strengths, thus making their strengths useless.

In the beginner to intermediate stages in tennis, one of the strategies that's used very often is to "attack the weakness and break it down." At the higher levels in tennis, the weaknesses that a player has are heavily guarded and concentrated. These quotes explain that the player has to disperse the opponent's concentration by attacking various parts of the court that are not heavily defended. It's only natural to guard a weaker side and by using this against the opponent, it can expose their weaknesses even further to be able to attack their weakness when it's left open.

e) Attack and defend against one's expectations

LI = measurement for distance. 1 LI equals to 0.25 miles

> "For should the enemy strengthen his front, he will weaken his rear; should he strengthen his rear, he will weaken his front; should he strengthen his left, he will weaken his right; should he strengthen his right, he will weaken his left. If he sends reinforcements everywhere, he will everywhere be weak. Numerical weakness comes from having to prepare against several possible attacks; numerical strength comes from compelling our adversary to make these preparations against us. Knowing the place and the time of the coming battle, we may concentrate from the greatest distances in order to fight. But if neither time nor place be known, then the left wing will be impotent to succor the right, the right equally impotent to succor the left, the front unable to relieve the rear, or the rear to support the front. How much more so if the furthest portions of the army are anything under a hundred LI apart, and even the nearest are separated by several LI! Though according to my estimate the soldiers of Yueh exceed our own in number, that shall advantage them nothing in the matter of victory. I say then that victory can be achieved. Though the enemy be stronger in numbers, we may prevent him from fighting. Scheme so as to discover his plans and the likelihood of their success."

[Translation]

The opponent can have more weapons, but if you can keep them busy by attacking them where it is unexpected, then victory can be achieved. It is best to minimize defending as much as possible. Meaning you're trying to make your opponent uncomfortable with every shot you hit. By making the opponent uncomfortable, it is possible to make them over hit and pressure themselves even more. Although having many weapons can be advantageous for a player, the number of weapons a player has cannot be concluded that they have a higher percentage of winning. It's the ability to use their weapons head-on and deceptively in different situations to attack, neutralize, and defend that defines a great player.

Direct and indirect methods, attacking, counterpunching, baiting the opponent, revealing weaknesses, attacking the strength to open up the weakness, tricking the opponent and moving them to where you want them. Ball striking ability of the player, mental focus, psychological games, physical endurance, strength, speed. Tennis is basically a chess match on steroids. One mistake can turn a point won into a point lost. Win or lose a point at any moment. It can be fun to watch the top players battling it out even without knowing these aspects of the game, but watching tennis knowing these strategical games and trying to analyze the player's intentions can be super addicting. It can also help tennis fans learn to appreciate tennis by realizing all the work that is done on the court.

f) Four ways to analyze the enemy's strengths and weaknesses

> *"Rouse him, and learn the principle of his activity or inactivity. Force him to reveal himself, so as to find out his vulnerable spots. Carefully compare the opposing army with your own, so that you may know where strength is superabundant and where it is deficient. In making tactical dispositions, the highest pitch you can attain is to conceal them; conceal your dispositions, and you will be safe from the prying of the subtlest spies, from the machinations of the wisest brains. Even if the victory was achieved in front of the multitude of eyes by corresponding well to the enemy's tactics – what many can't comprehend is how they achieved victory. All men can see the tactics whereby I conquer, but what none can see is the strategy out of which victory is evolved. Do not repeat the tactics which have gained you one victory, but let your methods be regulated by the infinite variety of circumstances."*

[Translation]

People think we have won because of our physical dispositions and the methods of attack, but they cannot see that the physical dispositions and the methods of attack were developed for victory. Sun Tzu is saying that people watching can tell that they won because they are good at fighting, but they have no idea how the analysis and the calculation was made to adapt to the opponent. The tactics are made by these factors during the match and every match has to be analyzed and adapted differently by that day's particular circumstances of the match.

The four factors are:

1 策之 – Measuring the positives and negatives of oneself and opponent's possible options
2 作之 – Purposely giving information to shake and disturb the opponent
3 形之 – Calculating places to attack and defend by the court positioning of oneself and the opponent
4 角之 – Testing the abilities of the opponent

With these four factors, which are mostly covered in the previous sections in this chapter, the player can focus on attacking the opponent's weaknesses. All of these factors can change faintly or moderately according to the conditions of the player and the opponent and how the point, game, or match is being played by both players. Since these circumstances can change every match, every match has to be approached somewhat differently even if the player has to play the same opponent from a previous tournament. Pre-match calculations can be made, but no one other than the player that is playing the match can truly know how the match has to be played out. When the opponent is defeated, the opponent is probably analyzing why and how they lost, but in actuality they should not know why. And because the calculations are made to defeat the opponent in circumstances of each match, the last phrase can be understood. "Do not repeat the tactics which have gained you one victory, but let your methods be regulated by the infinite variety of circumstances."

Although most of the strategy in *The Art of War* is based on deception and variations, after testing the opponent, if their strength is not as powerful as the player's strengths, the player can play to the opponent's strength and still achieve victory comfortably. Another way to defeat an opponent that is definitely lower level than the player is to copy the opponent's moves by letting them know "anything you can do, I can do better." This strategy is useful to break the opponent down quickly to have them mentally accept defeat during the match. These tactics can be interpreted as using direct maneuvers in relation to warfare.

g) Resembling the nature of water

> *"Military tactics are like to water; for water in its natural course runs away from high places and hastens downwards. So in war, the way is to avoid what is strong and to strike at what is weak. Water shapes its course according to the nature of the ground over which it flows; the soldiers works out his victory in relation to the foe whom he is facing. Therefore, just as water retains no constant shape, so in warfare there are no constant conditions. He who can modify his tactics in relation to his opponent and thereby succeed in winning, may be called a heaven-born captain. The five elements (water, fire, wood, metal, earth) are not always equally predominant; the four seasons make way for each other in turn. There are short days and long; the moon has its periods of waning and waxing."*

[Translation]

Tactics are compared to water because water can change its shape and form to accommodate all forms. The form of water can change, but the content does not change. The meaning of this passage is that "flexibility in tactics" has no definite shape or form, and it must be changed according to the situations and the opponent. Each of the five elements (water, fire, wood, metal, and earth) can suppress one another and represents the never-ending cycle of what suppresses what element. Summarizing the three chapters of tactics, it can be simplified to: consistency – the base power of the rally balls and to look for the opportunity (Chapter 4), power (spin, pace, timing) – the ability and how to attack your opponents

(Chapter 5), and placement (shot placement, depth, height, angles) – is to keep your opponents guessing and to attack their weaknesses (Chapter 6). Consistency is a must for pro players, but the priority of power and placement can switch according to the situation and opponents. Chapter 10: Terrain will mention the basic details of when and how to use those shots and vulnerabilities according to the opponent's positions.

VII.

MILITARY MANEUVERS (軍爭) – TRAVELING FOR TOURNAMENTS

In ancient warfare, military maneuver (軍爭) was the act of trying to position themselves to gain an advantage against the enemy. This chapter is closely related to how the team should be preparing themselves when entering a tournament. Some of the subjects that are covered in this chapter are: what factors to look for when picking a tournament, how the coach should support their players when they are playing a match, how to conserve energy when preparing for tournaments, and how a player should get ready for a match. In the book *The Art of War*, this chapter is said to have introductory properties of the upcoming chapters of chapter 8: Variations and adaptations through chapter 11: Battlegrounds.

a) Easy route is the difficult route

> *"Generally in war, the general receives his commands from the sovereign. Having collected an army and concentrated his forces, he must blend and harmonize the different elements thereof before pitching his camp. After that, comes tactical maneuvering, than which there is nothing more difficult.*
>
> *The difficulty of tactical maneuvering consists in turning the long winding detours into the direct, and misfortune into gain. Thus, to take a long and circuitous route, after enticing the enemy out of the way, and though starting after him, to contrive to reach the goal before him, shows knowledge of the artifice of circuitous straight."*

[Translation]

The mentioned general in this quote is the tactical general of a country. Taking this into account, this passage can be translated into the art of picking the right events and tournaments for the player to participate in. Tactical maneuvering of an army can be translated into traveling for tournaments as a team of coach, trainer, player, and other staff members. Many things can happen while traveling and even when things are going as planned, traveling long distances away from home is never easy.

The passage explains that what seems to be a long and circuitous route might be the shortest way to get to a waypoint. Also turning any misfortune into gain. National tournaments, lower tier international tournaments, and lower tier pro tournaments all have strong and weak tournaments. This means that the players participating in a given tournament can be strong or weak depending on the environmental factors, tournaments going on before, during, and after the chosen tournament, which players participated in the prior year, and the overall flow of the movement of the players in that year. These factors can be analyzed and decided with the help of experienced coaches. Some tournaments that are weaker can be farther away than the stronger tournaments. Some of the weaker tournaments might not have the best environment. But if traveling farther isn't a problem and if the player can handle the bad environments of a tournament, picking weaker tournaments is not an embarrassing thing to do. The goal is to get enough points to be qualified to play in the higher tier tournaments. When playing at the higher tier tournaments, the player can gain more experience by playing against better players. There's no shame in picking winnable tournaments when the player is also developing their game to get better and not just to win tournaments.

b) Rushing to tournaments

LI = measurement for distance. 1 LI equals to 0.25 miles

> "Maneuvering with an army is advantageous; with an undisciplined multitude, most dangerous. If you set a fully equipped army in march in order to snatch an advantage, the chances are that you will be too late. On the other hand, to detach a flying column for the purpose involves the sacrifice of its baggage and stores. Thus, if you order your men to roll up their buff-coats, and make forced marches without halting day or night, covering double the usual distance at a stretch, doing a hundred LI in order to wrest an advantage, the leaders of all your three divisions will fall into the hands of the enemy. The agile and strong men will be in front, the jaded ones will fall behind, and on this plan only one-tenth of your army will reach its destination. If you march fifty LI in order to outmaneuver the enemy, you will lose the leader of your first division, and only half your force will reach the goal. If you march thirty LI with the same object, two-thirds of your army will arrive. We may take it then that an army without its baggage-train is lost; without provisions it is lost; without bases of supply it is lost."

[Translation]

This passage indicates that rushing to a waypoint can lead to separation of the army and leaving behind their supplies and such. This can be translated to when a team travels to a tournament without calculating the time needed to adjust to the new environment. When traveling for tournaments, there is some time needed for the player to get adjusted to the new environment. Jet lag, checking the tension of the stringing machine in that tournament, changes in the water, speed of the court, court surface, type of ball used in the tournament, and other important factors that need time to get adjusted to the new environment. Making a hasty decision and traveling to a tournament because it seems advantageous for the player without giving the team enough time to get adjusted would be a huge mistake. Make sure to travel enough days before the tournament for the player to be able to perform without any hindrance due to lack of preparation time.

This can relate to local tournaments as well. Parents and players often make the mistake of arriving at their match and tournaments just in time for their match. It is also important to arrive early to be able to warm up and be in the right mindset to play the match. Rushing into a match right after arriving at the site will force the player to get adjusted in the match. While the opponent might not be ready either, you won't get so lucky every match.

c) Wind, forest, fire, and mountain – the natural environmental elements

> "We cannot enter into alliances until we are acquainted with the designs of our neighbors. We are not fit to lead an army on the march unless we are familiar with the face of the country – its mountains and forests, its pitfalls and precipices, its marshes and swamps. We shall be unable to turn natural advantage to account unless we make use of local guides.
>
> So in war, practice dissimulation to set up your enemy and decide whether to concentrate or to divide your troops based on the circumstances. Let your rapidity be that of the wind, your compactness that of the forest. In raiding and plundering be like fire, in immovability like a mountain. Let your plans be dark and impenetrable as night, and when you move, fall like a thunderbolt. When you plunder a countryside, let the spoil be divided amongst your men; when you capture new territory, cut it up into allotments for the benefit of the soldiery. Ponder and deliberate before you make a move. He will conquer who has learnt the artifice of deviation. Such is the art of maneuvering."

[Translation]

When going into battle to face the enemy in their country, it is important to know the environmental factors that might need to be accounted for. The quote, *"We are not fit to lead an army on the march unless we are familiar with the face of the country—its mountains and forests, its pitfalls and precipices, its marshes and swamps,"* emphasizes the importance of knowing the environmental factors. Not only is it important to know what type of surface the courts are, it is also important to know some of the environmental conditions of the courts, tournament site, and the country (if traveling overseas).

The four elements in these passages are wind, forest, fire, and the mountains. Although it does not directly translate into tennis, these four elements will be translated into the elements that can help or hinder the player's performance. The elements can affect how a player should attack and defend during the course of the tournament. These factors must be taken into account before making decisions to travel to certain tournaments; if not, the decision to go to a tournament is quite reckless.

Wind – Some regions are naturally very windy or some tournaments are always very windy at that particular time of the year during the tournament.

Forest – Some tournament sites have lots of trees and the courts are covered by the trees at certain times of the day. For a stadium, the shadows might cover parts of the court. For courts in the city, the tall buildings will cast shadows over the courts.

Fire – Fire relates to the climate of the region. How hot or cold is the participating region? Humidity and the dryness of a region as well. Humid regions make the ball heavier and dry regions make the ball lighter and faster through the air.

Mountains – The elevation or altitude of a region. The lower regions make the ball heavier and the higher elevation makes the ball lighter and travel farther.

All of these factors can be discussed with the team and if the player or the parents are not very familiar with an area, the coach usually has past experiences that they can share with the team and vice versa.

d) Eye contact and signals from the coach

> *"The Book of Army Management says: On the field of battle, the spoken word does not carry far enough: hence the institution of gongs and drums. Nor can ordinary objects be seen clearly enough: hence the institution of banners and flags.*
>
> *Gongs and drums, banners and flags, are means whereby the ears and eyes of the host may be focused on one particular point. The host thus forming a single united body, is it impossible either for the brave to advance alone, or for the cowardly to retreat alone. This is the art of handling large masses of men.*
>
> *In night-fighting, then, make much use of signal-fires and drums, and in fighting by day, of flags and banners, as a means of influencing the ears and eyes of your army."*

[Translation]

Gongs, drums, banners, and flags can be translated into the signals from the coach. Although coaching is prohibited, signs of support can give a player a huge mental boost. In order for the signs to work, they must be positive reinforcements and the coach must have a good relationship with their player to be able to feel the coach's sincerity. It's left to the coach's decision to signal while their player is playing and they must know that if the signals are vague, it does not always help the player. The coaches also have to be careful not draw any attention and lose respect from the opposing players, parents, and coaches by making the signals very obvious that it's coaching. It is best to give positive signals to the players so they can feel the coach's support. Some players like to block out all outside feedback. If the players prefer to play without any support from the coach or parents, it is better to support them by keeping the emotions in check until the player feels comfortable and fully trusts the coach.

e) Governing one's spirits and energy to fight – biorhythm (治氣), mental toughness (治心), endurance (治力), circumstances (治變)

> "Our army can rob the spirits of the whole enemy army; a commander-in-chief can disturb the enemies mind. Now a soldier's spirit is keenest in the morning; by noonday it has begun to flag; and in the evening, his mind is bent only on returning to camp. A clever general, therefore, avoids an army when its spirit is keen, but attacks it when it is sluggish and inclined to return. This is the art of studying spirits. Disciplined and calm, to await the appearance of disorder and hubbub amongst the enemy:--this is the art of retaining self-possession. To be attacking the enemy while the enemy is still far from us, to wait at ease while the enemy is toiling and struggling, to be well-fed while the enemy is famished:--this is the art of retaining one's strength. To refrain from intercepting an enemy whose banners are in perfect order, to refrain from attacking an army drawn up in calm and confident array:-- this is the art of studying circumstances."

[Translation]

These passages can tell us how to preserve one's energy and fighting spirits before playing a match by translating the four arts to these factors.

Art of studying spirits (治氣) – Biorhythm
Art of retaining self-possession (治心) – Mental toughness
Art of retaining one's strength (治力) – Endurance

Art of studying circumstances (治變) – Adaptation to circumstances

Art of studying spirits can relate to the biorhythm of a player. In ancient times, energy was believed to be constantly changing by seasons. As it is with seasons, there are changes in energy throughout the day. Although Sun Tzu disapproved of attacking an enemy in the morning for various reasons, biorhythm of a player throughout the day can vary from player to player. Some players can feel more active (physically and mentally) in the morning while other players can feel more active at midday or night. By being self-aware of at what part of the day they are most active, they can prepare themselves differently. For example, if a player has trouble playing a match at 8:00 am in the morning because they feel like their body is not fully awake, the player must prepare themselves by waking up way before the match time and give enough time for their body to wake up. Waking up an hour or hour and a half before the match usually isn't enough time for the player to get prepared properly. Trying to find the best time to wake up can come from the player's own experiences and instructions from the coach.

The art of retaining self-possession or mental toughness comes from discipline. Without discipline, the player will not be able to mentally block out all the annoyances that are happening near the court or next to the courts. The player must not let environmental factors like people talking or music playing loudly from afar bother them. Do not expect a young player to be able to block out those negative influences from the start. It must be taught and be disciplined by the parents and the coach for them to be able to block those influences. If the parents or the coaches get irritated themselves by these factors, they will not be able to discipline or teach the player because they can sense that the parents or the coach gets irritated by those factors as well.

Art of retaining strength can relate to the player's endurance and overall sustainable energy on the court. Staying at a hotel or housing at a reasonable distance from where the tournament is being held, staying focused and rested while at the tournament site before a match, and eating at the right time, the right food, and the right portion to help the player digest their food, and having enough energy throughout the match is all very important.

The art of studying the circumstances is the readiness to adapt to the circumstances. The player has to expect the unexpected and the nerves that the players feel have to be controlled. When players are nervous, their body will feel very heavy; by warming up properly and sticking to their routines before matches, it will help them to get focused and be ready to battle as soon as the match starts.

f) Forbidden actions while in battle

> *"It is a military axiom not to advance uphill against the enemy, nor to oppose him when he comes downhill. Do not pursue an enemy who simulates flight; do not attack soldiers whose temper is keen. Do not swallow bait offered by the enemy. Do not interfere with an army that is returning home. When you surround an army, leave an outlet free. Do not press desperate foe too hard. Such is the art of warfare."*

[Translation]

Sun Tzu wrote about some of the obvious mistakes that should not be made like playing directly into the opponent's strengths and not knowing why you're losing. Not fighting the enemy when they are coming downhill seems like common sense, but sometimes generals do make simple mistakes.

Some of the less obvious mistakes are provoking an opponent when they thrive off of anger or aggravating actions from their opponents. Especially when a player has played tournaments several weeks in row, some mentally weak players are very eager to get back home. When the opponent is eager to get back home and is tanking or not trying very hard, do everything you can to put him/her away swiftly and do not provoke them, which will wake them up to fight in the match with a vengeance.

When there are several tournaments (ITFs and Futures) and when you know an opponent has not done very well in the first couple of tournaments, do not let your guard down based on the results in the past weeks. The player might be desperate to earn points or will try to do their best in the last few weeks of the tournament. Take note of what type of players they lost to in the past weeks, but do not assume that it will be an easy match judging solely by the results.

VIII.

VARIATIONS AND ADAPTATIONS (九變) – CHANGES IN TACTICS AND STRATEGIES

In the book The Art of War, this chapter is about adapting to circumstances when there's an urgent matter. It explains how to make decisions based on the current situation. Being able to make swift decisions and adapt is key to surviving.

Pro players rarely keep a losing strategy in the next set. If they keep a strategy from a losing set, then that is because they might have lost the set only because of a few shot selection errors or chose the right shot but weren't able to execute. If the player decides that the current set can't be won, changing the strategy usually happens before losing that set to get prepared for the upcoming set.

a) The art of war of varying plans

> "In war, the general receives his commands from the sovereign, collects his army and concentrates his forces. When in caved in grounds, do not encamp. In country where high roads intersect, join hands with your allies. Do not linger in dangerously isolated positions. In hemmed-in situations, you must resort to stratagem. In desperate position, you must fight. There are roads which must not be followed, armies which must be not attacked, towns which must not be besieged, positions which must not be contested, commands of the sovereign which must not be obeyed.
>
> The general who thoroughly understands the advantages that accompany variation of tactics knows how to handle his troops. The general who does not understand these, may be well acquainted with the configuration of the country, yet he will not be able to turn his knowledge to practical account. So, the student of war who is unversed in the art of war of varying his plans, even though he be acquainted with the Five Factors of a leadership (將) (wisdom, belief, righteousness, bravery, discipline), will fail to make the best use of his men."

[Translation]

We will be focusing on the phrase "*...commands of the sovereign which must not be obeyed.*" There are times when the coach and the player have to make judgments contrary to the parents' will or instructions. For a player, it is very important to listen to the coaches and the parents' directions and instructions made to the player when the player is very young and is still in the early stages of their development. As the young player matures into an individual and their fundamentals get solid, there are times when they should not obey the directions depending on the circumstances of a match. A player can do everything right before and during the match, but if they do not understand how to adapt to the variations happening throughout their match, they will have a tough time beating any opponents comfortably. When the players are given specific instructions before a match, the player will try to do their best to follow the specific instructions to meet the parents' or the coach's expectations. This is why a lot of parents are puzzled as to why the coach does not give a young player specific instructions to defeat their opponents. There are countless variations and circumstances that might change during a match and if the player's mind is not mature enough or flexible enough to handle and are able to translate the coach's words according to the changing circumstances, it is best to not give specific instructions. The ability to adapt and change based on rapidly changing circumstances in a match is what the player needs to obtain through experiences of wins and losses. The coach's job is to work on countless situations in training and trusting the player to make the right decisions of what, when, and how they will use their shots according to the situations in the match. The coaches are well aware of the fact that the theories and actual match play are very different and the player has to gain knowledge by experiencing it firsthand. So for the parents, it is very important to understand and respect the decisions of the coaches and the players have made, whether the decisions that were made were during traveling for tournaments or decisions that had to be made during the match. Parents don't have to get too offended or take the actions and decisions they have made personally.

b) Do not rely on the enemy's actions, but rely on your readiness to counter their actions

> *"Hence in the wise leader's plans, considerations of advantage and of disadvantage will be blended together. If our expectation of advantage be tempered in the way, we may succeed in accomplishing the essential part of our schemes. If, on the other hand, in the midst of difficulties we are always ready to seize an advantage, we may extricate ourselves from misfortune. Reduce the hostile chiefs by inflicting damage on them; and make trouble for them, and keep them constantly engaged; hold out specious allurements, and make them rush to any given point. The art of war teaches us to rely not on the likelihood of the enemy's not coming, but on our own readiness to receive him; not on the chance of his not attacking, but rather on the fact that we have made them unable to attack."*

[Translation]

The first passage, *"Hence in the wise leader's plans, considerations of advantage and of disadvantage will be blended together..."* can tell us that with every decision or shot selection, both advantages and disadvantages must be thought through. One can pre-calculate on how an opponent will react to their actions, but it does not always go as smoothly as the player might think. The player must not expect any actions from the opponent to be as concrete as their own thoughts and take that into account while anticipating their opponents' moves. This can be understood as the supplementary explanation of the chapter, Weaknesses and Strengths, that a weakness can be used as a strength.

The last passage, *"The art of war teaches us to rely not on the likelihood of the enemy's not coming, but on our own readiness to receive him..."* emphasizes doing everything you can in training to maximize your strengths and reinforcing your weaknesses. Warming up properly and being in the right mindset before a match to get ready to adapt to any circumstances and to counter your opponents' strategies and tactics.

The second half of the passage, *"...not on the chance of his not attacking, but rather on the fact that we have made them unable to attack."* means in order for a player to prevent the opponent from attacking, they have to be strong and skilled enough themselves to make the opponents have a tough time attacking them. Once the player is able to handle different types of situations and shots, they will be able to trust themselves and be confident going into any match.

This is also why it's important to keep improving a player's game even after turning pro. The player must be stubborn enough to keep their weapons and abilities intact while trying to learn new shots or skills to be able to handle different types of opponents and situations. Being content with the level or with a ranking will stop the player from developing even further and make it impossible to climb up higher in the rankings. The player must learn to take a step backwards to take two steps forward.

c) Five dangerous faults of a general

> *"There are five dangerous faults which may affect a general:*
>
> *1 Recklessness, which leads to destruction;*
> *2 cowardice, which leads to capture;*
> *3 a hasty temper, which can be provoked by insults;*
> *4 a delicacy of honor which is sensitive to shame;*
> *5 over-solicitude for his men, which exposes him to worry and trouble.*
>
> *These are the five besetting sins of a general, ruinous to the conduct of war. When an army is overthrown and its leader slain, the cause will surely be found among these five dangerous faults. Let them be a subject of meditation."*

[Translation]

The five dangerous faults are the contrary notion of the Five Factors of a Good Leader in chapter 1: Initial Calculations, Section b), which explains the qualifications of a good general. These faults are all self-explanatory and they can all harm the players' ability to make clear and precise decisions to dominate their opponents. Like an experienced general in war, the player must possess a balanced and stable mindset. They must not be single-minded and selfish in their actions.

Recklessness can happen when a player is overly aggressive and cause too many unforced errors, which will hand over the match to the opponent. The player must be aggressive but not reckless. Some players understand being aggressive is to be reckless. Wisdom to understand the concept of how to be aggressive has to be taught and experienced through successes and failures.

Being cowardly and avoiding the fight and whining is only admitting defeat.

Having a short fuse will give your opponents a chance to provoke you and control you.

Caring too much for respect can hinder the player's ability to express their killer instincts on the court and care too much about how people judge them based on their actions.

Worrying too much about the outcome of the match without taking definitive actions will only bring hesitation and create weaknesses that the opponent can capitalize and dictate.

IX.

MOVEMENT OF THE ARMY (行軍) – MOVEMENT OF THE PLAYER AND THE TEAM

The direct translation of the title in this chapter is military march. This chapter's concept includes all of the movements of the army including maneuvering, battling, marching, and ways to station the army. This can translate into the movement of the player during a match and the overall actions and the movement of the team.

Footwork and stance would also be in this category for the actual movement of the player. Footwork and stance are like using different stances in martial arts. Different stances like bear, tiger, cat, or crane are used in different situations. The player must be able to adapt to the changes and learn how to move correctly if their natural abilities do not allow them to move correctly for tennis.

Fitness and fast feet are required for obvious reasons, but having fast feet is not the only key to moving well on the court. Moving well on the court means to be able to anticipate and read the opponent's moves as well as move and position themselves correctly according to the type of surface they are playing.

Although there are many technical details that can be added into this chapter, it will only explain the overall concept of the movement for the player and the team.

a) Tactics to attack according to the opponent's court positioning

> "We come now to the question of encamping the army, and observing signs of the enemy. Pass quickly over mountains, and keep in the neighborhood of valleys. Camp in high places, facing the sun. Do not climb heights in order to fight. So much for mountain warfare.
>
> After crossing a river, you should get far away from it. When an invading force crosses a river in its onward march, do not advance to meet it in mid-stream. It will be best to let half the army get across, and then deliver your9hyb attack. If you anxious to fight, you should not go meet the invader near a river which he has to cross. Moor your craft higher up than the enemy, and facing the sun. Do not move up-stream to meet the enemy. So much for river warfare.
>
> In crossing salt-marshes, your sole concern should be to get over them quickly, without any delay. If forced to fight in a salt-marsh, you should have water and grass near you, and get your back to a clump of trees. So much for operations in salt-marches.

> *In dry, level country, take up an easily accessible position with rising ground to your right and on your rear, so that the danger may be in front, and safety lie behind. So much for campaigning in flat country.*
>
> *These are the four useful branches of military knowledge which enabled the Yellow Emperor to vanquish four several sovereigns."*

[Translation]

The first sentence of the passage suggests encamping the army and observing the enemy. Encamping as a whole is understood as moving the army, stationing the army, and deploying the army. While encamping the army, the general must observe the enemy to make moves according to the terrain. This can relate to tennis as observing the position of the opponent along the baseline and the player positioning themselves according to the positioning of the opponent. After positioning themselves correctly, the player must hit the right shots into the correct zones of the court to make the opponent uncomfortable.

The figures in this section are to help players realize the opponent's positions, how to position and move themselves according to the opponent's position, and how to attack them according to their position. The general court positioning of the opponent can change depending on the situations of the match and the player should notice the changes as soon as possible to attack them accordingly.

Before the player can play according to the opponent's position on court and the situation they are in, the coach and the parents must ask whether they are able to perform these tasks. Did they practice or have enough experience with the type of opponent or type of style they must play to defeat the opponent? Is the player's mind flexible enough for them to actually deploy these strategies? Also the tactics and strategies in this section and the first section in Chapter 10 do not work if the opponent is overpowering the player. When the player is getting overpowered in the rally, they must be able to absorb the opponent's power or return the power back to the opponent; then once they have a chance to attack, they can attack to the specific zones in the court to make them feel as uncomfortable as possible.

General lateral court positioning

These examples are when the two players are on the baseline regardless of the depth of their position. The goal is to bisect the angles of the best possible shots of the opponent to be able to cover both sides. If the opponent does not have a good angle shot, crosscourt, or down the line, then the player should position themselves accordingly.

A = Player's Position
B = Opponent's Position

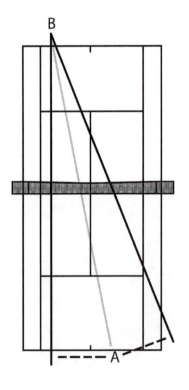

When hit to the Deuce Court

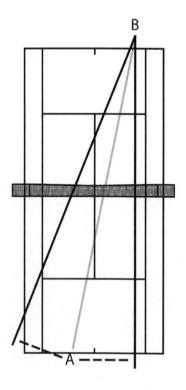

When hit to the Ad Court

Changes in lateral court positioning

Lateral court positioning can change when a player hits a big shot that is difficult to control for the opponent or if the opponent is on full sprint across the court to retrieve a shot. Notice Player A's court positioning is slightly different from the previous position. Player B is sprinting slightly away from the baseline; thus Player B has a higher chance of hitting the ball into the shaded area. Although circumstances can change by the speed of Player B and the ability to hit on the run, Player A should anticipate the opponent's move to attack accordingly.

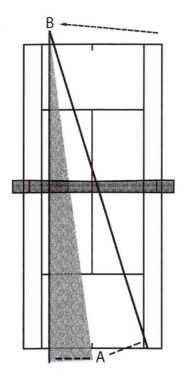 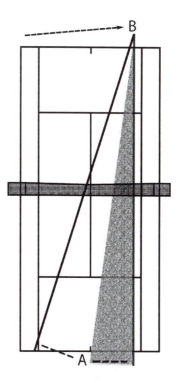

Against an opponent that generally hits on the rise on the baseline

The shaded area on the side of Player B is the target zone when the opportunity arises to attack or set up the point. Players that hit on the rise in general do not like backing up even when they have to defend. Hitting high and heavy into the shown area will force the opponent to hit on the rise on a tough deep ball with lots of spin. Notice Player A's position and the movement on the baseline. The player must be able to hit back the opponent's shots that are hit on the rise; then once they have a chance to attack, they must hit deep to force an error or a short ball to be able to attack.

Positioning and target zone

The shaded area in the player's view shows the recommended height to hit deep with heavy topspin to force the opponent to hit on the rise on a tough ball.

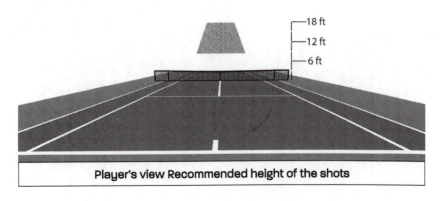

Player's view Recommended height of the shots

Against an opponent that generally likes to stay far behind the baseline

The shaded area near the sideline on the side of Player B is the target zone when the opportunity arises to attack or set up the point. The goal is to stretch them as much as possible to open up the court or bring them near the baseline to be able to attack them with depth as well as angles. Slice is effective against these types of players to bring them in near or inside the baseline, which forces them to play on top of the baseline or get caught near the no-man's land. Notice the positioning and the movement of Player A. Since opponents that play behind the baseline usually hit with topspin and depth, Player A must be able to position himself slightly further behind the baseline and be ready to move in when the ball lands short.

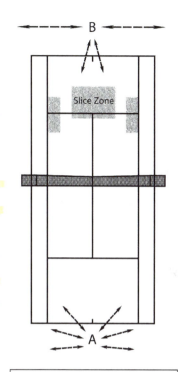

Positioning and target zone

The shaded areas in the player's view show the height recommended when the ball crosses the net to hit angles and slices effectively. By hitting the airzones, the player can stretch the opponent further out wide or to bring them forward.

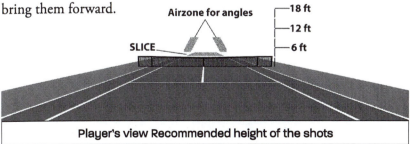

Player's view Recommended height of the shots

Against an opponent who positions themselves neutral

When the opponent is able to move freely up and back from the baseline, then the player must be able to hit the shaded areas according to the opponent's position and situations. Strategy is needed according to the opponent's ability.

Since these types of opponents are very versatile in most situations, the player should test their opponents by hitting deceptive high short balls that are not easy to attack or low slices to see what type of balls they like to attack on or have trouble with. High balls that land in the no-man's land when hit correctly are not easy to finish the point; the

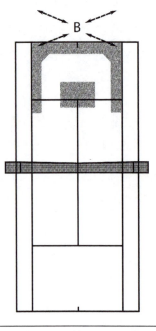

Positioning and target zone

player should watch how the opponent handles this particular shot and other shots depending on the situation to figure out what type of ball they prefer to hit.

Surprisingly, even some of the lower-ranked pros have trouble hitting the high ball and low sliced balls effectively. This can be used to bait other types of players as well.

Testing opponent to observe how they handle high or low balls

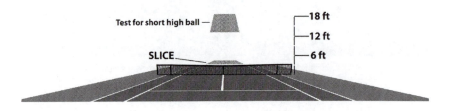

Approaching the net with an obvious approach shot

When Player A has to go into the net by hitting an approach shot, the goal is to hit the approach shot as big and effective (enough pace, spin, and depth) as possible to force the opponent to hit to the shaded area regardless of which direction the approach shot was hit.

If Player A was able to hit the approach shot effectively, then their positioning at the net is closer to the sideline in the direction the ball was hit (Position 1) since Player B does not have many options.

If Player A was not able to hit an effective approach shot, then the positioning at the net should be more towards the middle of the court to bisect the angles of the opponent's shot (Position 2). Player A must try to anticipate the opponent's passing shots by trying to read the movements of the opponent.

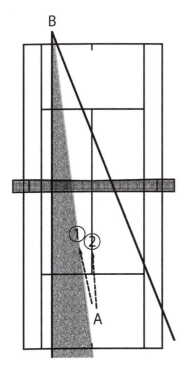
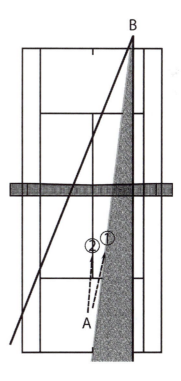

Returning against a serve and volleyer

The following figures show the returner's position and the zones to attack the return against a serve and volleyer. Notice how the returner must move in to take the serve on the rise to take away time against the serve and volleyer to close the net. Since hitting deep down the middle of the court gives the volleyer the best chance to attack and limits the time the returner can recover to the middle of the court, it is best to hit the return low down at their feet if the player can't control the return to hit down the line or an angle crosscourt.

If the serve and the first volley is not enough to finish the point, the player hitting the passing shots has too many options and it makes it tough for the serve and volleyer to cover the court. Just as it is with any strategy, if the opponent is faced with similar moves (serve and volleying in this instance) every point, they will look to counter the strategy at a critical moment. Given the zones of margin for error of the serve, the options for the volleys, and the options the passer has, shown in the first section of Chapter 10, it requires maximum mental focus, quickness in feet and decisions, and extremely accurate shots to serve and volley every point. It is best to serve and volley after analyzing the opponent's pattern of returns, then come in behind a serve to surprise the returner unless the surface is extremely fast.

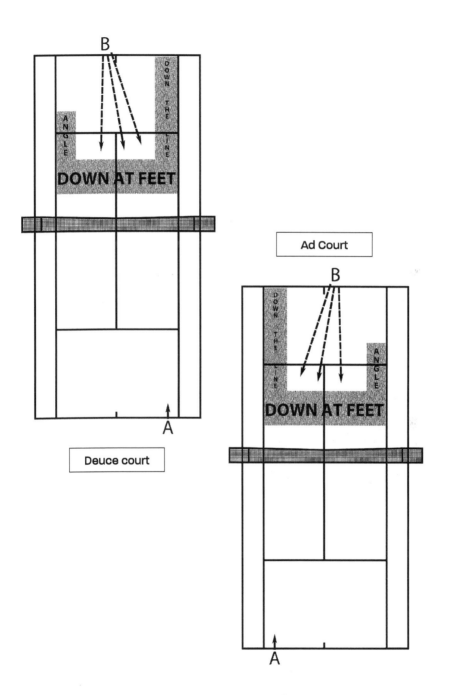

Second serve return position
– on the rise (Contact point 1)

The figure shows Player A moving in to hit the second serve (kick serve) on the rise before the ball goes above the optimal contact point. **The shaded area is the no-man's land for the second serve returns since it's an area where the ball peaks after the initial bounce and players should try not to hit the second serve in this area.**

The side view of the second serve path shows the optimal height the returns should be hit. To hit the return on the rise, the player must move forward inside the baseline. Depending on the height of the player, the optimal contact point can change higher or lower, but the concept of moving in does not change.

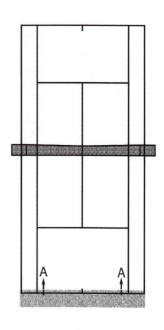

Return position

Side view of the second serve path and return height

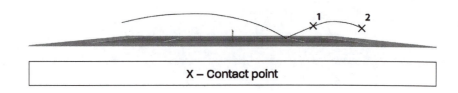

X – Contact point

Second serve return position
– letting the ball drop (Contact point 2)

The figure shows Player A moving back to hit the second serve (kick serve) on the rise before the ball goes above the optimal contact point. The player can prepare themselves in the shaded area to hide the strategy to move back. **The shaded area is the no-man's land for the second serve returns since it's an area where the ball peaks after the initial bounce and players should try not to hit the second serve in this area.**

The opponent may serve and volley if they notice that Player A is going to move back to hit the return consistently.

The side view of the second serve path shows the contact point when the ball is hit on the way down after the peak.

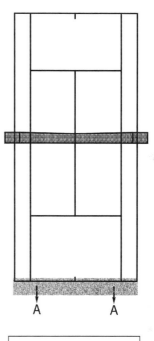

Return position

Side view of the second serve path and return height

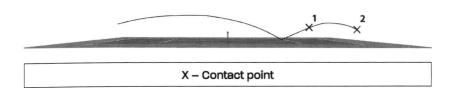

X – Contact point

Pros and cons of hitting the second serve returns on the rise or letting it drop

On the rise – Contact Point 1

Pros:
1) Less recovery time for the server
2) Hitting early can pressure the server without too much focus on placement and power.
3) Can make less experienced servers nervous on their second serves.
4) Can end points quickly. Fast-paced points. Less taxing on the body.
5) Takes away the option to serve and volley

Cons:
1) Miss hitting the returns – difficult to time
2) Requires more concentration in a shorter amount of time
3) If the return is short, there's no time to recover for the next shot
4) Positioned inside the baseline in the no-man's land after return.
5) Less recovery time to recover to the center of the court behind the baseline.

Letting the ball drop – Contact Point 2

Pros:
1) More time to load up to hit big or with heavy spin
2) More room to hit – margin for error (depth)
3) Server cannot all-out attack the next ball

4) More time to recover after the return

Cons:
1) Returns can land short because of how far the returner is standing
2) If used consistently, the server will not feel any pressure by timing
3) Can lose timing to hit returns on the rise.
4) Has to be placed deep in the corners or precise to be an attack
5) Long points. Taxing on the body.
6) Gives the option for the opponent to serve and volley as a surprise attack

b) Checking the players for injury and overall health

> "All armies prefer high ground to low and sunny places to dark. If you are careful of your men, and camp on hard ground, the army will be free from disease of every kind, and this will spell victory.
>
> When you come to a hill or a bank, occupy the sunny side, with the slope on your right rear. Thus you will at once act for the benefit of your soldiers and utilize the natural advantages of the ground.
>
> When, in consequence of heavy rains up-country, a river which you wish to ford is swollen and flecked with foam, you must wait until it subsides."

[Translation]

The army in ancient times needed to stay in sunny places for hygiene and sanitary purposes. Sun Tzu considered the natural advantages for the sake of the army's health. Coaches need to take the player's health into consideration when making decisions. The type of food they eat, change of water in different countries, adequate room temperature in their rooms, and other factors need to be constantly checked without nagging the players. Checking for any sign of injuries or overall health is different from being soft on them. The coach needs to have experience with common pain and soreness associated with training, changing equipment, or working on a specific movement. The player must play through aches and soreness, but if the player is feeling sharp pain, they must stop and take care of the issue.

c) No-man's land

> *"Country in which there are precipitous cliffs with torrents running between, deep natural hollows, confined places, tangled thickets, quagmires and crevasses, should be left with all possible speed and not approached. While we keep away from such places, we should get the enemy to approach them; while we face them, we should let the enemy have them on his rear.*
>
> *If in the neighborhood of your camp there should be any hilly country, ponds surrounded by aquatic grass, hollow basins filled with reeds, or woods with thick undergrowth, they must be carefully routed out and searched; for these are places where men in ambush or insidious spies are likely to be lurking."*

[Translation]

This phrase is about the land that the army should avoid and get out of as soon as possible. This can be interpreted into the no-man's land in tennis. It is the same principle as the dangerous lands in this phrase as it is okay to pass, but the player must move through or out of the no-man's land as it is very easy to get attacked in this zone. The player that is in the no-man's land can get attacked at all locations of the player's court.

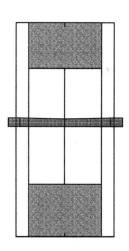

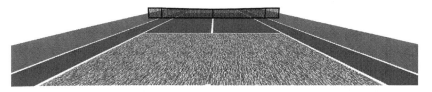

d) 33 movements of the enemy

"When the enemy is close at hand and remains quiet, he is relying on the natural strength of his position.

When he keeps aloof and tries to provoke a battle, he is anxious for the other side to advance.

If his place of encampment is easy of access, he is tendering a bait.

Movement amongst the trees of a forest shows that the enemy is advancing. The appearance of a number of screens in the midst of thick grass means that the enemy wants to make us suspicious.

The rising of birds in their flight is the sign of an ambuscade. Startled beasts indicate that a sudden attack is coming.

When there is dust rising in a high column, it is the sign of chariots advancing; when the dust is low, but spread over a wide area, it betokens the approach of infantry. When it branches out in different directions, it shows that parties have been sent to collect firewood. A few clouds of dust moving to and fro signify that the army is encamping.

Humble words and increased preparations are signs that the enemy is about to advance. Violent language and driving forward as if to the attack are signs that he will retreat.

When the light chariots come out first and take up a position on the wings, it is a sign that the enemy is forming for battle.

Peace proposals unaccompanied by a sworn covenant indicate a plot.

When there is much running about and the soldiers fall into rank, it means that the critical moment has come.

When some are seen advancing and some retreating, it is a lure.

When the soldiers stand leaning on their spears, they are faint from want of food.

If those who are sent to draw water begin by drinking themselves, the army is suffering from thirst.

If the enemy sees an advantage to be gained and makes no effort to secure it, the soldiers are exhausted.

If birds gather on any spot, it is unoccupied. Clamor by night betokens nervousness.

If there is disturbance in the camp, the general's authority is weak.

If the banners and flags are shifted about, sedition is afoot.

If the officers are angry, it means that the men are weary.

> *When an army feeds its horses with grain and kills its cattle for food, and when the men do not hang their cooking-pots over the camp-fires, showing that they will not return to their tents, you may know that they are determined to fight to the death.*
>
> *The sight of men whispering together in small knots or speaking in subdued tones points to disaffection amongst the rank and file.*
>
> *Too frequent rewards signify that the enemy is at the end of his resources; too many punishments betray a condition of dire distress.*
>
> *When envoys are sent with compliments in their mouths, it is a sign that the enemy wishes for a truce.*
>
> *If the enemy's troops march up angrily and remain facing ours for a long time without either joining battle or taking themselves off again, the situation is one that demands great vigilance and circumspection."*

[Translation]

In this passage, there are 33 movements and activities to look for when facing the enemy to understand their intentions before and during the battle. Sun Tzu is stating that the enemy's external behavior can be observed to figure out the enemy's situation. Even the slightest movement of the enemy can be used to anticipate and help plan an attack. When the players are observing the opponent before and during the match, these are some of the movements that they can bear in mind to anticipate the opponent's moves.

a) Changing their grip on the run to a continental with their back straight on the run on the backhand side means that they cannot attack but are still able to control the shot.

b) Changing their grip on the run to a continental with their back turned or leaning forward on the run on the backhand side means that they are not in control and they are on the defensive.

c) Changing their grip on the run to a continental with the racket back high and legs doing a split on their forehand side means that they are on defense but are still able to control the shot. Low slice may be hit back to you.

d) Changing their grip on the run to a continental with the racket back low and legs doing a split on their forehand side means that they are not able to control the shot and will pop the ball up.

e) If the opponent is panting with their mouth open without playing a long point, it means that they are nervous or they are not used to the situation.

f) If the opponent puts their hands on their knees to rest in between the points, it means that they are physically worn.

g) When the opponent looks at their parents or coach after losing a point, it means that they are unsure of themselves.

h) When the opponent is staring at the next court, then it means that they are not really into the match. When the score is close, they might be losing their concentration; if they are winning by a big margin, then they might be looking just to put you down.

i) When they scream "come on" unusually loudly after hitting a winner on a less important point, it means that they are unsure if the shot hit was in or out.

j) When the opponent argues with the chair umpire or the referee for an obvious call, it means that the opponent is taking a physical or a mental break from the match.

k) If the opponent takes an unusually big racket back on a short ball or an approach shot, it may mean that the opponent will be hitting a drop shot.

l) When an approach shot or a volley is hit to the opponent's backhand side and the opponent is leaning back on their back foot, it means that they are going to hit a lob.

m) Opponents with big backswings might have trouble hitting low fast-paced balls and are limited by the backswing to hit on the rise effectively but are good at hitting slower easy balls and hitting high heavy balls.

n) Opponents with compact backswings might have trouble hitting back high heavy deep balls but are good at changing directions and hitting on the rise.

o) Opponents who play way behind the baseline do not like to attack first and usually do not like to come in to the net.

p) Opponents who play on top of the baseline like to hit on the rise, but they usually lack the ability to add height and heavy spin to the ball.

q) Opponents who position themselves towards the backhand side in between points either like to hit around their backhand and/or they are covering their weaker backhand.

r) When opponents position themselves in the center of the court on the baseline, in relation to the sidelines, that means that they like to hit their backhand and trust in their backhand to be just as aggressive as their forehand. They also might like to hit down the line backhands more than other players.

s) Loose body language usually means that they lose their temper faster and/or do not care as much.

t) Good posture and stable movements usually mean that they are mentally strong.

u) If the opponent smiles at any point of the match, then it means that they are mentally loose at the moment.

v) If the opponent constantly gets mad at themselves, it means that they always get mad at themselves and it does not mean that they are about to break down.

w) Players that are shorter than the average height usually are used to long rallies; players that are taller than average are used to keeping the points shorter.

x) The average walking speed of the opponent in between points relates to their patience or the lack of patience during a point. Slower means patient and faster means impatient.

y) If the opponent is tossing the ball multiple times before they serve, they are feeling the nerves or they are not confident in their serve.

z) The model and the brand of the racket they are using can help determine what type of game style they might have before going into the match.

aa) If the opponent looks hurt or injured during a match but is playing out the point, the opponent is over acting to distract you and the pain is bearable. Concentrate on making them suffer.

bb) In between the points, if the opponent stands very still fighting the pain of an injury, then they might be in real pain and might forfeit the match.

cc) If the opponent charges in to the net a lot more frequently than usual without hitting a great approach shot, it means that the opponent is feeling that they cannot beat you from the baseline in any way and trying to change the strategy.

dd) If the opponent starts pushing the ball high and stays consistent, they want you to lose patience and go for shots that are not right to attack.

ee) If the opponent resorts to extreme measures that are not their usual game like hitting moon balls or slapping the ball on every shot, it means that they are mentally gone and it is their last resort. Fight them off for the last time and they will be put away.

ff) If the opponent is rustling and unrested on the change-over, it means that in the next game, they will most likely be rushing on the first couple of points.

gg) If the opponent is stretching or massaging themselves during the change-over, it means that they have some kind of pain that is bothering them.

hh) If the opponent seems too nice throughout the match, it means that they are hiding their true intentions. Expect to be surprised at critical moments.

A smart player will not only be able to recognize and anticipate opponent's moves, but as their opponent's level gets higher, they are able to reverse the use of these signs to confuse opponents and use it against them.

e) Do not underestimate and do not be afraid

> *"If our troops are no more in number than the enemy, that is amply sufficient; it only means that no direct attack can be made. What we can do is simply to concentrate all our available strength, keep a close watch on the enemy, and obtain reinforcements. He who exercises no forethought but makes light of his opponents is sure to be captured by them."*

[Translation]

This passage explains that even if the enemy's troops outnumber our troops, it is enough to defeat the enemy by using stratagem. It is not a matter of how many weapons and troops they have; it is a matter of proficiency of the combat general to control and use the weapons at the right times. When the enemy is outnumbering our troops, directly attacking the enemy is reckless. Concentrate on attacking with all available weapons and neutralize the opponent by observing their strengths and anticipating their moves.

The opponent can be a better player when comparing them to our player shot by shot, but if the shots cannot be strung together to build the point, there are plenty of chances to defeat the opponent. The objective of a match at a higher level is to win the match, not to show off who has more weapons or better shots. Different types of shots must be worked on when the player is developing, but once the developing stage of a player has passed, it is important to find ways to defeat the opponent no matter how good their opponent is.

f) The coach /player relationship – not too close, not too distant

> *"If soldiers are punished before they have grown attached to you, they will not prove submissive; and, unless submissive, then will be practically useless. If, when the soldiers have become attached to you, punishments are not enforced, they will still be useless. There for soldiers must be treated in the first instance with humanity, but kept under control by means of iron discipline. This is a certain road to victory. If in training soldiers commands are habitually enforced, the army will be well-disciplined; if not, its discipline will be bad. If a general shows confidence in his men but always insists on his orders being obeyed, the gain will be mutual."*

[Translation]

This passage focuses the importance on obtaining authority in training and leadership. In Chinese, the character 親 which is sense of closeness, is repeatedly used in this passage. In order for the coach to instruct and convince players to follow their lead, the coach must respect the player as a person and treat them with kindness. In order for the coach to discipline and punish the player, the coach must not be too close to the player as it might emotionally and mentally hurt the player or it can give the player a reason to grieve when the player receives a punishment; nor should the coaches be too distant and strict to the player as they might not obey the coach deep down. In other words, the player can act like they are obeying the coach on the surface level, but will remain disobedient on the inside.

This is the reason why the coach should not start coaching the players as soon as they start working together. The player has to know the coach and the coach has to know the player. It might even take a couple of weeks for the coach to actually be able to coach the player and give instructions on the court. It is the coach's job to make the player comfortable enough to have them share their thoughts on tennis and other general thoughts about life. Once they have mutual respect for each other, the synergy effect of having a coach can truly see the light.

As discussed in the earlier chapters, if the parents interfere with the coach/player relationship on the court, off the court, and at home, the coach will not have the complete respect from the player. It is the parent's job to always respect the coach on court, off court, and more importantly, at home when the coach is not present.

X.

TERRAIN (地形) – ZONES OF THE COURT

This chapter is about the topographical features discussed in the book *The Art of War*. Not only does it cover the actual characteristics of land, but it explains the psychological state of the soldiers in certain areas of terrain. In tennis, this can translate into the zones of the court and the surface of the court. Although the surface tennis is played can be divided into three major surfaces (hard court, clay court, and grass), the chemicals, materials, and layers used to surface the courts can change the way they play significantly. The ITF has a long list of court pace classifications, which are divided into five categories ranging from slow to fast, on their website to explain how fast the court plays depending on the materials.

The first section of this chapter will be about the zones of the court. Some of the zones that this chapter will cover are: places that can be attacked, zones of the serve, zones of the returns, and other zones to help players use according to their situations during a point. The sections following the initial section may be irrelevant to the zones of the court, but are translated in terms of how they should be understood relating to tennis.

a) Attack zones of the court

> *"We may distinguish six kinds of terrain, to wit: (1) Accessible ground; (2) entangling ground; (3) temporizing ground; (4) narrow passes; (5) precipitous heights; (6) positions at a great distance from the enemy.*
>
> *Ground which can be freely traversed by both sides is called accessible. With regard to ground of this nature, be before the enemy in occupying the raised and sunny spots, and carefully guard your line of supplies. Then you will be able to fight with advantage.*
>
> *Ground which can be abandoned but is hard to re-occupy is called entangling. From a position of this sort, if the enemy is unprepared, you may sally forth and defeat him. But if the enemy is prepared for your coming, and you fail to defeat him, then, return being impossible, disaster will ensue.*
>
> *When the position is such that neither side will gain by making the first move, it is called temporizing ground. In a position of this sort, even though the enemy should offer us an attractive bait, it will be advisable not to stir forth, but rather to retreat, thus enticing the enemy in his turn; then, when part of his army has come out, we may deliver our attack with advantage.*
>
> *With regard to narrow passes, if you can occupy them first, let them be strongly garrisoned and await the advent of the enemy. Should the army forestall you in occupying a pass, do*

not go after him if the pass is fully garrisoned, but only if it is weakly garrisoned.

With regard to precipitous heights, if you are beforehand with your adversary, you should occupy the raised and sunny spots, and there wait for him to come up. If the enemy has occupied them before you, do not follow him, but retreat and try to entice him away.

If you are situated at a great distance from the enemy, and the strength of the two armies is equal, it is not easy to provoke a battle, and fighting will be to your disadvantage.

These six are the principles connected with Earth. The general who has attained a responsible post must be careful to study them."

[Translation]

In this section, the terrain and the grounds will be translated into the zones of the court. The zones are marked to help players realize where to attack or place the ball rather than the positioning of the player. The main differences to the first section in Chapter 9 are that these tactics do not reflect the changes in the player or the opponent's positioning. It will show the best zones to attack on the court and the shot selection the player has in certain situations.

The attack zones can also help parents and spectators understand how small the zones and the targets are in order for a player to be able to dictate the opponent on a certain shot. Knowing that these zones are not very big, people can appreciate more when they watch the performances of pro players at the highest level.

Most of the figures shown in this section depict a situation in which both players are right-handed. When a left-handed player plays a right-hander or if both players are left-handed, the circumstances can change.

Best zones to attack regardless of height and spin

The shaded zones at the corner of the baseline and the sideline can be attacked with low flat shots with pace or high and heavy topspin regardless of where the player is positioned.

The shaded zones where the sideline meets the service line can be attacked with a crosscourt angle shot or inside-in forehand.

The shaded zones where the net and the sideline meet are the placement for the drop shots or angle volleys.

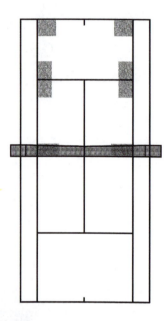

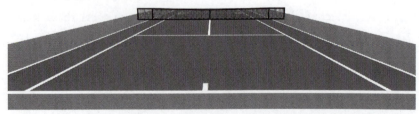

The player's view is shown to inform parents and spectators how small the targets are in order for the players to dictate with placement. Pro players can usually feel where the ball is going to land as soon as the ball leaves the strings rather than visually checking where the ball is landing.

First serve zones

The shaded zones shown in these figures show the zones where the server can hit their first serve to give them the best chance to dictate. Notice the differences in the paths of the ball for a right-handed player and left-handed player.

If the first serve is **hit inside the shaded zones**, then the player can get ready to attack with the shot after the serve.

If the first serve is **hit in between the shaded zones**, no matter how fast the serve, the returner will have a higher chance to counter attack with a return. If the first serve is hit in between the shaded zones, the server must stay alert as the returner might attack with their returns.

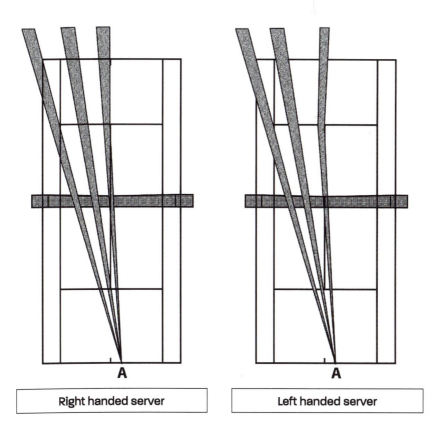

| Right handed server | Left handed server |

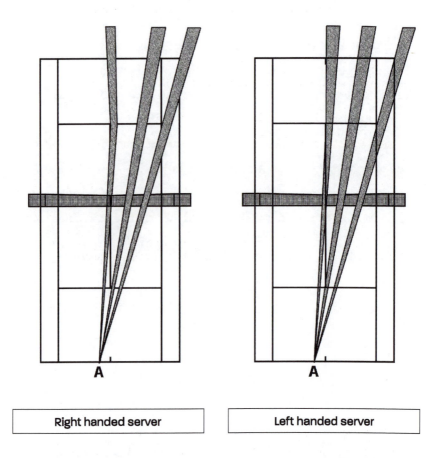

| Right handed server | Left handed server |

The speed of the serve is an important factor in hitting an effective serve, but since most pro players can add decent pace to their serve, speed will not be mentioned. Another factor that can change is the pattern of the serves. Most players other than the best servers have favorite placements for their serves at certain situations in a match. If the serves are not mixed up to keep the returner guessing, they will be able to anticipate and attack on the return.

First serve return zones – Deuce court

This figure shows the zones to attack the returns when hit with a normal topspin return. Slice zones are not shown in this figure.

The figure is showing Player A (right-handed player) hitting a forehand return. The shaded area is the optimal placement for the returns. When the return is hit inside the shaded area with enough pace, the returner can start out playing the point by dictating or neutralizing the server.

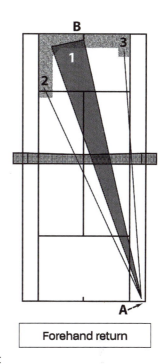

Forehand return

Zone 1 marked on the side of Player B is the safest placement for the returner. When the ball is hit with enough pace in Zone 1, the returner can quickly bisect the angles of the server after the return as it is more difficult for the server to direct the shot to the open court.

Target 2 can be hit when the first serve is slightly slower than expected, which makes the returner hit early and is able to hit an angular return to attack the server.

Target 3 is the riskiest out of the three return zones. If the return is hit slightly short of the shaded zone in Target 3, the server can dictate easily by hitting the ball early on the rise or hit a sharp angle shot to the open crosscourt. The returner can also hit to Target 3 while aiming the return at Zone 1 when they are slightly late on the return. The returner must recover immediately to cover the open court after the return is hit.

This figure is showing Player A (right-handed player) hitting a backhand return.

The shaded area slightly changes when hitting a backhand return since the position of Player A is in the middle of the court after hitting the return.

Zone 1 marked on the side of Player B is the safest placement for the returner. Again, if the return is hit into Zone 1, the returner can cover the open court by bisecting the angles for the server. If Player B has a weaker backhand, then it adds to the advantage for Player A. Also if the return is hit deep into Zone 1, it makes it tougher for Player B to hit a sharp crosscourt shot to the open court.

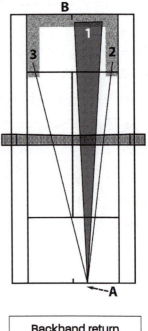

Backhand return

Target 2 can be hit when the first serve is slightly slower than expected, which makes the returner hit early and is able to hit closer to the sideline to start the point.

Target 3 is the toughest return to successfully hit on purpose for the returner if it is their backhand return. Most of the time, the returner will hit this target when they are late in hitting the return. If this shot is not hit with enough pace or depth, the returner can get attacked very easily with a crosscourt angle or a down the line shot.

First serve return zones – Ad court

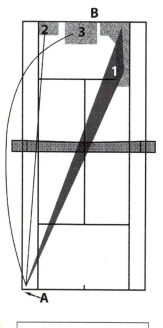

Backhand return

The zones in this figure show the options for the returner.

The figure is showing Player A (right-handed player) hitting a backhand return. The shaded area is the optimal placement for the returns. When the return is hit inside the shaded area with enough pace, the returner can start out playing the point by dictating or neutralizing the server.

Zone 1 should be the standard placement to hit a backhand return on the ad side since it takes less recovery time to bisect the angles of the server on the next shot. Also if the return is placed in the shaded area of Zone 1, the returner has more options to attack the third ball after the serve by hitting behind the opponent while they are recovering to the middle, hit to the open court to the deuce side, or by hitting a dropshot to the deuce court.

Target 2 can be hit when the returner is stretched out wide but still has control over their shot. If the returner gets stretched out wide on their backhand return, it is difficult for them to hit an effective crosscourt return and the only option would be to go down the line. Target 2 can be hit when the returner is late but because the angle of hitting down the line is still at an angle towards the middle of the court, the return is barely late. When the return is short while trying to hit Target 2, the server has a huge advantage on the next shot.

Target 3 for the backhand return can be hit with pace to attack the return or with height if the returner cannot attack the return. When hitting with pace, the returner has to hit with enough power to jam the server to limit their ability to control the direction of the shot. When hitting the return at Target 3 with height to buy some time to recover to the middle of the court, the return should not be too high because it gives the server a chance to serve and volley. If the return has to be hit high into Target 3, it should be hit extremely high with a continental grip to force the server to stay on the baseline.

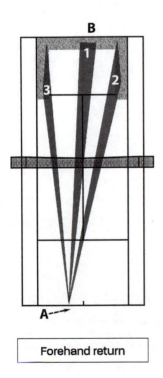

Forehand return

This figure is showing Player A (right-handed player) hitting a forehand return. The shaded area is the optimal placement for the returns. When the return is hit inside the shaded area with enough pace, the returner can start out playing the point by dictating or neutralizing the server.

This figure shows the forehand return placement zones for the ad court. Notice how the options are marked as zones rather than targets. If Player A is a right-handed player, the chances are very high that they can attack their forehand return to any of the three zones. Some exceptions are when the returner has an extreme western grip or if the backswing is needlessly huge, limiting them to hit an effective return.

Hitting to **Zone 1** can jam the server on the next shot if it is hit with enough pace.

Hitting to **Zone 2** can set up the next shot to force the server to hit down the middle.

Hitting early to **Zone 3** can take away time since the distance is shorter than hitting down the middle or crosscourt into Zone 2.

Basic options of the volleyer

The farther away the volleyer is from the net, the less margin there is for hitting an effective volley to put the opponent in trouble. The volleyer has the advantage by taking time away from the opponent, but the volleyer has to stay alert because if the volley is not precisely placed, the opponent will be given too many options to pass the volleyer.

Zone 1 can be hit behind the service line.

Zone 2 can be hit as well as **Zone 1** as the player closes in to the net to hit a deep volley, an angle volley, or a drop volley. Players should try to hit the approach shot well enough or sneak in to the net to close in as much as possible to finish the point effectively.

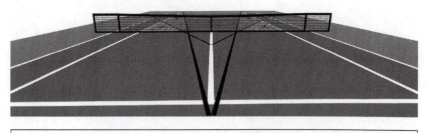

Player's view Recommended height of the shots

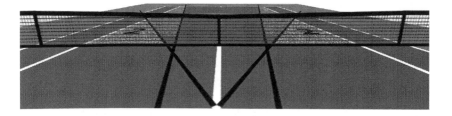

Player's view Recommended height of the shots

Zones to hit passing shots

The zones indicated in the two figures show the options for the passer, Player A. The numbers indicate the difficulty according to the speed of the approach shot hit by Player B. Fastest being 1 and slowest being 6. The slower the approach shot, the more options the passer has.

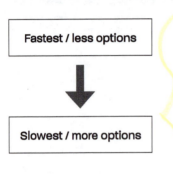

1. Big shot directly at the volleyer
2. Passing shot down the line
3. Topspin shot down at the volleyer's feet
4. Touch shot low at the volleyer's feet
5. Angle shot crosscourt
6. Topspin lob over the volleyer

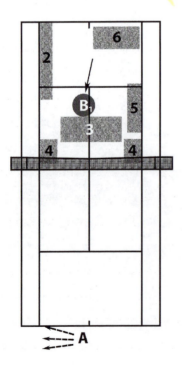
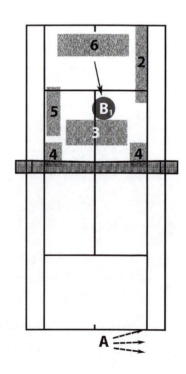

1. **Big shot directly at the volleyer** – If the approach shot is too powerful to do anything, the best option is to go big right at the opponent's body to take away any angles and try to pass on the next shot.
2. **Passing shot down the line** – The down the line can be hit on the rise before the opponent is able to come in close to the net to cover the line. If the down the line pass is not taken on the rise, then the opponent will have time to close in to the net, which makes the target much smaller. Try to hit on the rise before the opponent can split step.
3. **Topspin shot down at the volleyer's feet** – When the pass is hit down at the feet, the opponent has to hit a drop volley or pop the ball up to hit deep. This will give the passer enough time to react to the volleyer. This is especially useful when Player A can sense that Player B has not closed in to the net fast enough or is stationed farther away from the net on the first volley.
4. **Touch shot low at the volleyer's feet** – The goal of this shot is to make the volleyer hit a drop volley. As soon as Player A hits a touch shot to Zone 4, they need to start moving in and stay alert to cover the drop volley. In order for Player A to hit the touch shot to Zone 4, the pace of the approach shot has to be somewhat faster because of the time the touch shot takes to travel to Zone 4. If the approach shot was slow and Player A hits a touch shot to Zone 4, Player B will have enough time to come in all the way in to the net to finish the point.
5. **Angle shot crosscourt** – Angle shot can be hit if the approach shot is slower and Player B is able to move in to the net closer and cover the line. Another instance Player A can hit crosscourt for a pass is when Player B is coming in to the net after an approach shot from

the outside of the sideline towards the middle of the court. When this is the case, Player A needs to hit the pass on the rise to lessen the time Player B can cover for the crosscourt pass.

6. **Topspin lob over the volleyer** – When Player B hits an approach shot that does not have much pace and Player A is moving towards the back fence to hit the pass, Player A can hit a lob over Player B. Since the approach shot is slow, Player B has more time to close in to the net, which makes it easier for the lob to be successful.

Player's view on the Ad side

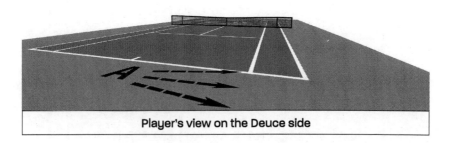
Player's view on the Deuce side

The player's view is shown to inform parents and spectators how small the targets are in order for the players to dictate with placement. Pro players can usually feel where the ball is going to land as soon as the ball leaves the strings rather than visually checking where the ball is landing.

Zones to hit when retrieving drop shots

When Player B hits a drop shot, in most cases, Player A has three options. The numbers indicating the three options are labeled based on how much feel is needed to successfully hit the shot. Option 1 requiring less feel and firmer wrist and Option 3 requiring the most feel and detailed control of the wrist.

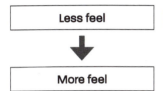

1. Deep down the line (farthest in distance)
2. Angle crosscourt
3. Drop shot in front of the net (closest in distance)

Depending on Player A's ability (or lack of ability) to hit touch shots, Player B can anticipate which zone Player A can retrieve successfully.

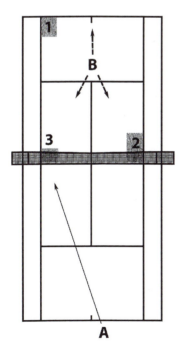 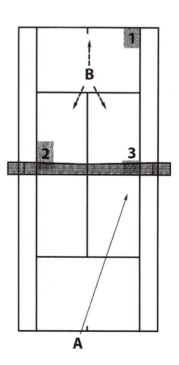

Player's view when retrieving drop shots on the Ad court

The airzones are marked along the net to give an idea of where to aim depending on which zones they want to hit.

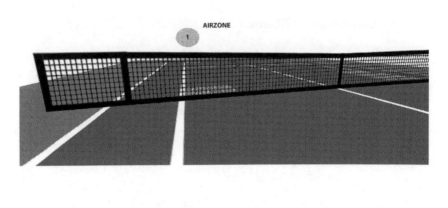

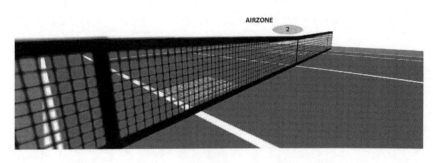

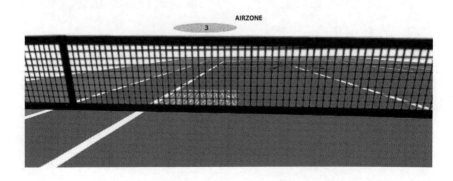

Player's view when retrieving drop shots on the Deuce court

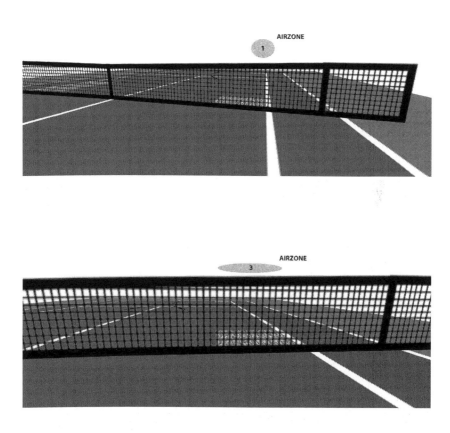

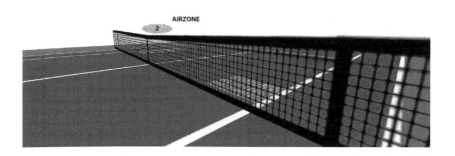

b) Six types of faults leading to defeat

"Now as army is exposed to six several calamities, not arising from natural causes, but from faults for which the general is responsible. These are: (1) Charge; (2) insubordination; (3) collapse; (4) ruin; (5) disorganization; (6) rout.

Other conditions being equal, if one force is hurled against another ten times its size, the result will be the flight of the former.

When the common soldiers are too strong and their officers too weak, the result is insubordination.

When the officers are too strong and the common soldiers too weak, the result is collapse.

When the higher officers are angry and insubordinate, and on meeting the enemy give battle on their own account from a feeling of resentment, before the commander-in-chief can tell whether or not he is in a position to fight, the result is ruin.

When the general is weak and without authority; when his order are not clear and distinct; when there are no fixes duties assigned to officers and men, and the ranks are formed in a slovenly haphazard manner, the result is utter disorganization.

When a general, unable to estimate the enemy's strength, allows an inferior force to engage a larger one, or hurls a weak detachment against a powerful one, and neglects to place

> *picked soldiers in the front rank, the result must be rout.*
>
> *These are six ways of courting defeat, which must be carefully noted by the general who has attained a responsible post."*

[Translation]

This section is closely related to Chapter 9: Variations and Adaptations, Section c). If the previous section was about the natural character of the general that can lead them to failure, this section is about the mistakes that can be made during the battle that can lead to a loss.

1) *Charge* – Is when the player is being reckless in a match. Being overly aggressive or hitting shots that are very low percentage.

2) *Insubordination* – Is when the player has the shots but is fragile mentally. The player is not mature (or disciplined) enough or has not been taught to use their mental strength to use the shots properly.

3) *Collapse* – Is when the player is mentally tough but does not have the shots to defeat the opponent. Not enough training to improve the quality of the shots.

4) *Ruin* – Is when the player is angry at the parents or coach and acts solely on bad emotions. The player is getting back at anyone who cares about their tennis by ruining the match.

5) *Disorganization* – Is when the player hesitates during the match on their shot selection and any decision during the match.

6) *Rout* – Is when the player is using a strategy that helps the opponent more than the player themselves.

c) It is not a matter of who is right or wrong

> *"The natural formation of the country is the soldier's best ally; but a power of estimating the adversary, of controlling the forces of victory, and of shrewdly calculating difficulties, dangers and distances, constitutes the test of a great general. He who knows these things, and in fighting puts his knowledge into practice, will win his battles. He who knows them not, nor practices them, will surely be defeated. If fighting is sure to result in victory, then you must fight, even though the ruler forbid it; if fighting will not result in victory, then you must not fight even at the ruler's bidding. The general who advances without coveting fame and retreats without fearing disgrace, whose only thought is to protect his country and do good service for his sovereign, is the jewel of the kingdom."*

[Translation]

This section is related to the section in Chapter 9: Variations and Adaptation, Section a). The passage, *"If fighting is sure to result in victory, then you must fight, even though the ruler forbid it; if fighting will not result in victory, then you must not fight even at the ruler's bidding,"* again emphasizes how important it is for the combat general to make decisions to fight even if it is against the king and the tactical general's orders if the general is sure of victory; and if the battle will surely be lost, then it is up to the combat general to decide not to fight for the sake of the kingdom. When working as a team, the parents, coach, and the player must work together to achieve victory. When the player is playing a match, it is their decision to deploy a strategy that will work on the opponent. Although it can be frustrating to see the player play with a strategy other than the strategy the parents had in mind, the player is not trying to disrespect the parents by deploying a different strategy if the opponent's weakness is absolutely transparent to the player. Unless the coach points out that it was the wrong strategy to deploy, the parents must try to understand that the circumstances in the match can change. As long as the player means no disrespect to the parents and the coach and is doing whatever they can to win the battle, it is up to them to decide.

d) Warmhearted but being strict to the player

> *"Regard your soldiers as your children, and they will follow you into the deepest valleys; look upon them as your own beloved sons, and they will stand by you even unto death. If however, you are indulgent, but unable to make your authority felt; kind-hearted, but unable to enforce your commands; and incapable, moreover, of quelling disorder: then your soldiers must be likened to spoilt children; they are useless for any practical purpose."*

[Translation]

The soldiers in this phrase will be referred to as players for better interpretation. Since the player is the parents' child, this can be understood very well for the parents. If the players are spoiled by lenient parents and coaches, they will not be of practical purpose. In other words, the player will become egotistical and conceited by the generosity of the parents and the coaches. The purpose is to help the player become the best that they can be, but if warmhearted discipline is absent, then the player will not be able to develop self-discipline and battle against many opponents, which will make their life miserable on the court. As mentioned in an earlier chapter, in order for the coach to be able to discipline the player, the coach must be close enough to the player in order for the player to understand the purpose of the disciplinary actions.

e) Know thyself, know thy enemy and know the environment

> *"If we know that our own men are in a condition to attack, but are unaware that the enemy is not open to attack, we have gone only halfway towards victory. If we know that the enemy is open to attack, but are unaware that our own men are not in a condition to attack, we have gone only halfway towards victory. If we know that the enemy is open to attack, and also know that our men are in a condition to attack, but are unaware that the nature of the ground makes fighting impracticable, we have still gone only halfway towards victory. Hence the experienced soldier, once in motion, is never bewildered; once he has broken camp, he is never at a loss. Hence the saying: If you know the enemy and know yourself, your victory will not stand in doubt; if you know Heaven and know Earth, you may make your victory complete."*

[Translation]

One of Sun Tzu's most famous quotes is in this passage: *"If you know the enemy and know yourself, your victory will not stand in doubt; if you know Heaven and know Earth, you may make your victory complete (知彼知己 知天知地).*" Not only do you have to know the enemy and yourself, but the characteristics of the court and the variables and circumstances of the environment have to be used to the player's advantage. Heaven and earth are not only the environment, but they can be interpreted as everything other than the opponent.

The three instances that lower the chances of winning are:

1. Knowing one's strength but not the opponent.
2. Knowing opponent's strength but not thyself.
3. Knowing one's strength but not the characteristics of the court and the variables of the environment.

XI.

NINE BATTLEGROUNDS (九地) – SCORING SYSTEM AND POINT MANAGEMENT

Most sections in this chapter of the actual book The Art of War, other than the first section, do not have a clear correlation with other sections in the chapter. Regardless of this inconsistency, it does have useful words of wisdom to consider that could be applied to the field of tennis.

In regard to tennis, the focus in this chapter will be mostly about the point system and point management. The score can also be considered to be the grounds on which the game is played. Just as in warfare, which battlegrounds has to be considered to be able to fight according to the configurations, the score in the points, game score, and the set score have to also be taken into consideration to deploy a certain strategy and tactics or use the opponent's tendencies in certain situations of the score in a game against them.

The scoring system in tennis is very cruel and unforgiving. When an error is made, the player gives the opponent a point, unlike many other popular sports. Every time a point is played, the player either gains a point or the opponent gains a point. To an extreme extent, the point system is understood as either kill or be killed. A string of misses can put a player in a horrible situation in a game. It is quite understandable why so many young players get passive when playing a match. It is not easy to break the fear of losing or giving a point to the opponent with an error. Some of the top pros make this mistake and they constantly have to remind themselves to be aggressive. You do not get rewarded for hitting great shots, but you do get penalized for hitting an error, which is why even the most aggressive players in practice have trouble finding their safe but aggressive range in a match.

One of the most interesting and exciting aspects about the scoring system in tennis is the score DEUCE in a game. Although it might be physically taxing for the players, the score DEUCE represents the power struggle between two players trying to get the advantage in the battleground. By taking away DEUCE in a game, the game becomes even more cruel and passive by not allowing any mistakes and it ends the game with a single deciding point.

For these reasons, players need to carefully manage how they use the score to use certain strategies or use reverse psychology on the opponents to gain ground.

a) The nine grounds and point management

"The art of war recognizes nine varieties of ground:

(1) Dispersive ground

(2) Facile ground

(3) Contentious ground

(4) Open ground

(5) Ground of intersecting highways

(6) Serious ground

(7) Difficult ground

(8) Hemmed-in ground

(9) Desperate ground

When a chieftain is fighting in his own territory, it is dispersive ground. When he has penetrated into hostile territory, but to no great distance, it is facile ground. Ground the possession of which imports great advantage to either side, is contentious ground. Ground on which each side has liberty of movement is open ground. Ground which forms the key to three contiguous states, so that he who occupies it first has most of the Empire at his command, is a ground of intersecting highways. When an army has penetrated into the heart of a hostile country, leaving a number of fortified cities in its rear, it is serious ground. Mountain forests, rugged steeps, marshes and fens — all country that is hard to traverse: this is difficult ground. Ground which is reached through narrow gorges, and from which we can only retire by tortuous paths, so that a small number of the enemy would suffice to crush

> *a large body of our men: this is hemmed in ground. Ground on which we can only be saved from destruction by fighting without delay, is desperate ground.*
>
> *On dispersive ground, therefore, fight not. On facile ground, halt not. On contentious ground, attack not. On open ground, do not try to block the enemy's way. On the ground of intersecting highways, join hands with your allies. On serious ground, gather in plunder. In difficult ground, keep steadily on the march. On hemmed-in ground, resort to stratagem. On desperate ground, fight."*

[Translation]

Sun Tzu is using the grounds on which the army is positioned to explain the differences in the strategic movements on nine different types of grounds. This can relate to how a player should be playing generally according to the situation and the grounds on which the score stands. Although for the audience, it can look like each point is played the same way, the feeling and the situation the player is in as it relates to the score in a game are very different for every point during the game. In respect to the nine grounds in the book *The Art of War*, the score in a game will be divided into nine similar situations the server faces for relativity.

1. **Dispersive ground** – First point of the game; 0-0 and 15-15
2. **Contentious ground** – Even score before game or break point; 30-30 and Deuce
3. **Facile ground** – One point up by the server; 15-0 and 30-15
4. **Ground of intersecting highways** – two points up by the server;

30-0

5. **Open ground** – One point down by the server; 0-15 and 15-30
6. **Difficult ground** – Two points down by the server; 0-30
7. **Serious ground** – Game point by the server; 40-0, 40-15, 40-30, Ad in
8. **Hemmed-in ground** – Break point for the opponent; 30-40 and Ad out
9. **Desperate ground** – Two or more break points; 15-40 and 0-40

The scores 0-0 or 15-15 can be related to **dispersive ground** because it is the first point of the game and when the server and the returners score, they are in equal conditions.

The scores 30-30 or Deuce can be related to **contentious ground** because it is the point when either side can be in a clear advantage.

One point up or 15-0 and 30-15 can be related to **facile ground** because of the way the server should not relax and keep going even if they are up a point.

Two points up or 30-0 can be related to the **intersecting highways** because depending on the outcome of the point won or lost, it can considerably put the server in a different situation. If the point is won, the server is at a great advantage; if the point is lost, then the server is at facile ground.

One point down or 0-15 and 15-30 can be related to **open ground** because although the server is down in the score, having the advantage of the serve makes this ground more equal than it seems.

Two points down or 0-30 can be related to **difficult ground** because the server is in a difficult situation no matter how it's looked at.

Game points by the server or 40-0, 40-15, 40-30, and ad in can be related to **serious ground** because the server needs to steal the last point to end the game.

Break points for the opponent or 30-40 and ad out can be related to **hemmed–in ground** because the opponent is on advantageous grounds.

Two or more break points for the opponent or 0-40 and 15-40 can be related to **desperate ground** because the server needs to fight off multiple break points to even the score.

The interpretation of nine grounds is only to provide reference to what type of situation the player is in. The mental aspects of the grounds are further explained in section f) in this chapter.

b) Attacking what the opponent holds dear

> *"Those who were called skillful leaders of old knew how to drive a wedge between the enemy's front and rear; to prevent co-operation between his large and small divisions; to hinder the good troops from rescuing the bad, the officers from rallying their men. When the enemy's men were united, they managed to keep them in disorder. When it was to their advantage, they made a forward move; when otherwise, they stopped still. If asked how to cope with a great host of the enemy in orderly array and on the point of marching to the attack, I should say: "Begin by seizing something which your opponent holds dear; then he will be amenable to your will." Rapidity is the essence of war: take advantage of the enemy's unreadiness, make your way by unexpected routes, and attack unguarded spots."*

[Translation]

Sun Tzu is advising to keep the enemy in disarray, but what if the enemy is still organized? The answer is to attack something that is important to the enemy. In tennis, it can be interpreted as attacking or being prepared to counterattack the opponent's strengths. When the rally starts after the first two strikes (serve and the return), when the player has an opportunity to attack, instead of attacking the weaker side, they can attack the opponent's strength to counter their move to the weaker side. For a basic example, if the opponent likes to hit forehands or turn around the backhand side and hit forehands, the player can attack the opponent's forehand to neutralize their forehand (strength) first, then attack to their weaker side. The opponents usually don't expect someone to attack their strength, but when the opponents are observed carefully, the player can notice even their strengths can be exposed as a weakness if the player can test the opponent by adding pace, spin, height, hitting the ball early, or specific placement of a shot. Another instance is when the opponents like to serve to a specific spot on an important or specific point. The player can anticipate the opponent's favorite serve and attack the return to get a chance to neutralize the opponent's serve. Whatever the strategy may be, taking away the opponent's strength is key. This is primarily for when the score within a game is close or when the opponent is down. They will resort to patterns and shots they will feel most comfortable with. The player's job is to read the opponent's plan of attack and attack, counter-attack, or defend accordingly.

Whatever the plan might be, foot speed and positioning are the essence of tennis. Quickness of the player can catch the opponent off guard and can leave no options but to defend the player. This phrase can be applied to all times during the match because the speed and rapidity of the player is important throughout the match.

c) Managing the players to keep the right mindset when traveling

> *"The following are the principles to be observed by an invading force: The further you penetrate into a country, the greater will be the solidarity of your troops, and thus the defenders will not prevail against you. Make forays in fertile country in order to supply your army with food. Carefully study the well-being of your men, and do not overtax them. Concentrate your energy and hoard your strength. Keep your army continually on the move, and devise unfathomable plans. Throw your soldiers into positions whence there is no escape, and they will prefer death to flight. If they will face death, there is nothing they may not achieve. Officers and men alike will put forth their uttermost strength. Soldiers when in desperate straits lose the sense of fear. If there is no place of refuge, they will stand firm. If they are in hostile country, they will show a stubborn front. If there is no help for it, they will fight hard. Thus, without waiting to be marshaled, the soldiers will be constantly on the qui vive; without waiting to be asked, they will do your will; without restrictions, they will be faithful; without giving orders, they can be trusted. Prohibit the taking of omens, and do away with superstitious doubts. Then, until death itself comes, no calamity need be feared. If our soldiers are not overburdened with money, it is not because they have a distaste for riches; if their lives are not unduly long, it is not because they are disinclined to longevity. On the day they are ordered out to battle, your soldiers may weep, those sitting up*

> *bedewing their garments, and those lying down letting the tears run down their cheeks. But let them once be brought to bay, and they will display the courage of a Chu or a Kuei."*

[Translation]

In controlling and managing the army, it is very important to keep the men in the correct mindset and in good health. Sometimes the coach and the parents must be bold and help the player to be able to compete because there's no choice but to survive, not because it is against the player's will. The first verse *"the further you penetrate into a country, the greater will be the solidarity of your troops, and thus the defenders will not prevail against you,"* can be related to tennis when the team travels to play a big event or a tournament. The player does not have to be told to be focused, eat healthy, train hard, and act professional. As the level of the tournament gets higher and the atmosphere around these big tournaments will keep the player focused.

As for the smaller and lower level tournaments, sometimes the players need to get set up in the position where they cannot retreat. In other words, the parents have the power to keep the player traveling until the player reaches a certain level or a ranking. If the goal of the player is to become a top pro and achieving that level has to be done anyway, then not giving them the option to come back home until they reach a certain ranking can be a motivating goal for the players. Although the player might not be too happy at first, they will soon realize that they have to focus and do whatever they can to reach that level. Having too many options will only feed doubt in the players' minds and by taking the options away, the players focus and concentrate on the task at hand. When the parents take action to take options away, the players need to understand that the parents are taking action to help them and have much belief in them.

d) Like the Shuai-jan, the snake

> "The skillful tactician may be likened to the shuai-jan. Now the shuai-jan is a snake that is found in the ChUng mountains. Strike at its head, and you will be attacked by its tail; strike at its tail, and you will be attacked by its head; strike at its middle, and you will be attacked by head and tail both. Asked if an army can be made to imitate the shuai-jan, I should answer, Yes. For the men of Wu and the men of Yueh are enemies; yet if they are crossing a river in the same boat and are caught by a storm, they will come to each other's assistance just as the left had helps the right.
>
> Hence it is not enough to put one's trust in the tethering of horses, and the burying of chariot wheels in the ground. The principle on which to manage an army is to set up one standard of courage which all must reach. How to make the best of both strong and weak — that is a question involving the proper use of ground. Thus the skillful general conducts his army just as though he were leading a single man, willy-nilly, by the hand."

[Translation]

The importance of this passage is in the unity of the army and the ability to control the army to attack the enemy in different ways. Since snakes are considered to be cunning and tricky, Sun Tzu has compared the controlling of the army to the acts of a snake. Every time the opponent changes their method of attack, the player must be able to attack the opponent in different ways according to the opponent's moves. One of the examples can be, if the opponent likes to hit on the rise, the player can back up behind the baseline and try to hit deeper and heavier (add more topspin) so the opponent has trouble hitting on the rise. If the opponent moves back trying to counter the heavy shot, then the player can use angles to punish the opponent for giving so much room. If the opponent tries to play steady and be consistent, then the player can use patterns and tactics to outplay the opponents. To deploy these strategies, the player must be able to hit all the shots needed in the strategy and unify them into one to be able to use them at will. In other words, knowing how to hit shot by shot does not mean anything if the shots cannot be connected together to form a complete pattern to finish the point.

e) Too much information for the players

> *"It is the business of a general to be quiet and thus ensure secrecy; upright and just, and thus maintain order. He must be able to mystify his officers and men by false reports and appearances, and thus keep them in total ignorance. By altering his arrangements and changing his plans, he keeps the enemy without definite knowledge. By shifting his camp and taking circuitous routes, he prevents the enemy from anticipating his purpose.*
>
> *At the critical moment, the leader of an army acts like one who has climbed up a height and then kicks away the ladder behind him. He carries his men deep into hostile territory before he shows his hand. He burns his boats and breaks his cooking-pots; like a shepherd driving a flock of sheep, he drives his men this way and that, and nothing knows whither he is going. To must his host and bring it into danger:—this may be termed the business of the general.*
>
> *The different measures suited to the nine varieties of ground; the expediency of aggressive or defensive tactics; and the fundamental laws of human nature: these are things that must most certainly be studied."*

[Translation]

Some of the coach's plans should be kept to themselves until the decisions of a plan are finalized. The player does not need to know every little detail, nor should they want to know much. Although too little information can be a problem as well, when the players are given too much detail for a certain decision or a move, the player will start doubting the coach's intentions if the coach makes it seem like there are frequent changes to their decisions. Sometimes the coach will seem to make an extreme or unreasonable decision to the inexperienced eye, but the coach does not only act upon current calculations and analysis, they act upon their past experiences and their intuitions as well. Communication between the coach and the player can be bilateral, but when a decision is made by the coach, the player should respect the coach's decision. The player will only trust the coach's decision without any doubts if the player has a sense of closeness and respect for the coach.

f) Different psychological state of the players by points

> "When invading hostile territory, the general principle is, that penetrating deeply brings cohesion; penetrating but a short way means dispersion. When you leave your own country behind, and take your army across neighborhood territory, you find yourself on critical ground. When there are means of communication on all four sides, the ground is one of intersecting highways. When you penetrate deeply into a country, it is serious ground. When you penetrate but a little way it is facile ground. When you have the enemy's strongholds on your rear, and narrow passes in front, it is hemmed-in ground. When there is no place of refuge at all, it is desperate ground. Therefore, on dispersive ground, I would inspire my men with unity of purpose. On facile ground, I would see that there is close connection between all parts of my army. On contentious ground, I would hurry up my rear. On open ground, I would keep a vigilant eye on my defenses. On ground of intersecting highways, I would consolidate my alliances. On serious ground, I would try to ensure a continuous stream of supplies. On difficult ground, I would keep pushing on along the road. On hemmed-in ground, I would block any way of retreat. On desperate ground, I would proclaim to my soldiers the hopelessness of saving their lives. For it is the soldier's disposition to offer an obstinate resistance when surrounded, to fight hard when he cannot help himself, and to obey promptly when he has fallen into danger."

[Translation]

The nine grounds of the battlefield are mentioned once again. Sun Tzu made use of the psychological state of the soldiers to fight differently according to the changes in the grounds. One example is when they are on desperate ground, the soldiers are told to fight till the last breath to be able to survive since there is no turning back.

Although improvising and adaptation to circumstances is key when the player is in critical situation based on the score, skilled players know exactly what they have to do to get out of danger by gut instincts. They've experienced getting out of trouble before and they remember the feeling of danger when down in score and activate their super focus. Skilled players also know the feeling and what mental state the returner is in when the returner is up in the score. By using total focus and the psychological tactics, they can get themselves out of trouble. By reversing and using the psychological tactics against the server, the player can effectively break the opponent's serve by anticipating the server's move.

The following are the basic psychological states of the server and the returner by score in a game:

1. **Dispersive ground** – First point of the game; 0-0 and 15-15

    Since it's very easy to think that there are still a lot of points left to win the game for both players, it is easy to start off the game casually. For this reason, it is important for the server to gather themselves and focus from the first point of the game. It sets the ground for the whole game and the first serve must be made to heighten the chances of winning the first point and the service game. At 15-15, the situation and the feeling of the server is similar to the start of the game.

2. **Contentious ground** – Even score before game or break point; 30-30 and Deuce

   At 30-30 or Deuce, either player can have an advantage if the point is won because the next point played is either a game point or break point. The server will feel the tension and pressure from the returner, so it is important to keep their concentration by not letting something influence them. The returner will be fighting very hard this point to win a break point from the server.

3. **Facile ground** – One point up by the server; 15-0 and 30-15

   At 15-0 or 30-15, it's easy for the server to feel relieved of the pressure of the score being even. The looseness of the server's mentality will result in an uncontrolled big first serve or a loose first serve error. The returner must be able to capitalize on the first serve error to even the score and keep the opponent pressured in the next point.

4. **Ground of intersecting highways** – two points up by the server; 30-0

   At 30-0, the server has a chance to turn this game into a real easy hold or potentially be a dog fight of a game. The server seems to be in control of the game, but if the point is lost, the returner still has a chance to even the score because of the looseness of the server's mentality at 30-15 if the server does not stay alert.

5. **Open ground** – One point down by the server; 0-15 and 15-30

   At 0-15 and 15-30, the returner seems like they have an advantage, but since the server still has the advantage of having the serve to start the point and the psychological state that the server will be in makes the grounds much more even than it seems. The server will do whatever they can to even the score. Which relates to defending the point with might. This would be the best time to gain a clear advantage for the returner by winning this point to demoralize the server.

6. **Difficult ground** – Two points down by the server; 0-30

At 0-30, the server will either be super focused or feeling demoralized by the disadvantageous grounds in the score. The server will quickly try to get themselves out of trouble with their big serve or resort to their best shot to win the point. For the server, it does not have to be mentioned how important it is to win this point. For the returner, they can over think or stay mentally loose in these situations, so they must be decisive and stay aggressive but not reckless to keep the server pressured. If the server has a big serve, then the returner must take a chance to attack all out on this point.

7. **Serious ground** – Game point by the server; 40-0, 40-15, 40-30, Ad in

The score at game point for the server will make them feel like they are so close to closing out the game and might leave an opening by thinking that the opponent will miss for them. The returner has nothing to lose and is not pressured at all since it's not their service game, so the returner will not back down easily. Do not relax and assume that the returner will miss. Unless the server closes out the game, the returner will always look to capitalize on the server's errors.

8. **Hemmed-in ground** – Break point for the opponent; 30-40 and Ad out

   Although the server is down a break point, the server is not feeling immense pressure on their first serve. The server will be alert from the moment they step up to hit their first serve and will focus on putting the first serve in, naturally. If they miss the first serve, the pressure is felt much greater. For the returner, they must decide quickly on how they want to play out the point when the first serve is missed, by attacking the server or neutralizing them to keep them pressured off of the second serve. Hesitation will only bring regrets. It is better to stay aggressive and attack than hesitate and make an unforced error.

9. **Desperate ground** – Two or more break points; 15-40 and 0-40

   Desperate grounds call for desperate measures. Since there is no room for error, the server must use their total concentration to get out of trouble. Although the score is advantageous for the returner, there will be lots of thoughts in the returner's head and their reflexes on their returns will be hindered by the many thoughts on both first and second serves. Capitalize on this psychological state and be strong. Stay aggressive on the serves to add even more pressure to the returner. For the returner, the added option to be less careful in their shot selection will leave them vulnerable. They must quickly decide how they will attack or neutralize the server. If the server has a pattern of placement when they are in trouble, they must notice the patterns and anticipate accordingly to capitalize on the obviousness of their serve.

g) Importance of point management

> "We cannot enter into alliance with neighboring princes until we are acquainted with their designs. We are not fit to lead an army on the march unless we are familiar with the face of the country – its mountains and forests, its pitfalls and precipices, its marshes and swamps. We shall be unable to turn natural advantages to account unless we make use of local guides. To be ignored of any one of the following four or five principles does not befit a warlike prince. When a warlike prince attacks a powerful state, his generalship shows itself in preventing the concentration of the enemy's forces. He overawes his opponents, and their allies are prevented from joining against him. Hence he does not strive to ally himself with all and sundry, nor does he foster the power of other states. He carries out his own secret designs, keeping his antagonists in awe. Thus he is able to capture their cities and overthrow their kingdoms. Bestow rewards without regard to rule, issue orders without regard to previous arrangements; and you will be able to handle a whole army as though you had to do with but a single man. Confront your soldiers with the deed itself; never let them know your design. When the outlook is bright, bring it before their eyes; but tell them nothing when the situation is gloomy. Place your army in deadly peril, and it will survive; plunge it into desperate straits, and it will come off in safety. For it is precisely when a force has fallen into harm's way that is capable of striking a blow for victory."

[Translation]

The importance of this passage is to know and understand the battlegrounds when maneuvering the army. If the grounds are interpreted into the score in this chapter, the importance is to know how to manage the score in points, games, and sets. Since knowing how to manage the score has to be done whoever the opponent is, the importance of the ability to manage points within a game cannot be emphasized enough.

h) Calmness of a maiden and rapidity of a running hare

> *"Success in warfare is gained by carefully accommodating ourselves to the enemy's purpose. By persistently hanging on the enemy's flank, we shall succeed in the long run in killing the commander-in-chief. This is called ability to accomplish a thing by sheer cunning. On the day that you take up your command, block the frontier passes, destroy the official tallies, and stop the passage of all emissaries. Be stern in the council-chamber, so that you may control the situation. If the enemy leaves a door open, you must rush in. Forestall your opponent by seizing what he holds dear, and subtly contrive to time his arrival on the ground. Walk in the path defined by rule, and accommodate yourself to the enemy until you can fight a decisive battle. At first, then, exhibit the coyness of a maiden, until the enemy gives you an opening; afterwards emulate the rapidity of a running hare, and it will be too late for the enemy to oppose you."*

[Translation]

When watching a match of two players, there are situations when the score within a game is always going to 30-30 or deuce, but one of the players ends up winning the game all the time. That might be because of the level difference, but in many cases it's because the player that has won the games can manage the points and plays according to the differences in the score. The player that has won the games might have stayed slightly passive to test the opponent, but at a crucial moment in the game score, they can pull out their A game and widen the score between the two players by attacking the player's weakness or by attacking the opponent with the analysis of how the player played up until 30-30 or deuce. When the score reaches 30-30 or deuce in a lot of the games with a higher ranked opponent, but the player cannot win any games, it can also mean that the player does not have an element of surprise on how they can attack the opponent if there is an opportunity given to the player. The player must take some calculated risks to attack the opponent to pressure the opponent.

XII.

ATTACKING WITH FIRE (火攻) – ANGER MANAGEMENT

This chapter introduces the application of fire in warfare. Since fire (火) also means anger or rage in Chinese, the translation will be about emotional attacks and dealing with emotions. Although fire was used widely and frequently in ancient warfare, Sun Tzu considered using fire as a last resort. Attacking with fire will not only damage the enemy, but if it's not used with caution, it can cause serious damage to the allies. As it is with war, using emotional attacks or provoking the enemy can do more harm than good to oneself if strict self-control is not laid in the core of the superficial delusions. Not everyone can use anger correctly as it is very easy to get consumed by the fire. Using emotional attacks is either berated or highly rated. Some rave about it, some despise it. The person on the receiving end of the emotional attacks will never be able to fully respect the player that is using the emotional attacks.

Using anger is not just to use it against your opponents, but channeling the negative energy within into positive energy can be considered using fire as well. How the emotional energy is used can be the difference between being a true champion or displaying unsportsmanlike conduct by whining and giving excuses to avoid their problems.

a) Handling different types of fire

> *"There are five ways of attacking with fire. The first is to burn soldiers in their camp; the second is to burn stores; the third is to burn baggage trains; the fourth is to burn arsenals and magazines; the fifth is to hurl dropping fire amongst the enemy.*
>
> *In order to carry out an attack, we must have means available. The material for raising fire should always be kept in readiness. There is a proper season for making attacks with fire, and special days for starting a conflagration. The proper season is when the weather is very dry; the special days are those when the moon is in the constellations of the Sieve, the Wall, the Wing or the Cross-bar; for these four are all days of rising wind."*

[Translation]
There are different events that can trigger anger.

(1) Anger towards self – technical and tactical errors
(2) Anger towards the opponent – cheating or annoying opponents
(3) Anger towards people – opponent's parents and the crowd

(4) Anger towards environment – linesmen/refs, wind, shadows, temperature, etc.

Anger towards oneself can be used to wake themselves up from making the same mistakes. If the problem and the solution is known but not executed, the player can get energy by telling themselves to execute properly. When the mistake is tactical or based on shot selection, the player can express themselves more freely than making a technical error. If a technical error is made, it is best to keep the emotions in check, so it does not give away the technical weaknesses to the opponent.

Being angry at an opponent because they are being unsportsmanlike or cheating can help the player to justify beating their opponents badly. Doing everything they can to defeat them and punishing them for their inappropriate and unfair actions.

Being angry at the people outside of the match can happen quite often. If the cause of the anger is the opponent's parents, the player needs to ignore them and shut them out completely. It is best not to counter their actions at all. By ignoring them, the opponent's parents will only feed off of their own fire and damage themselves.

There are two instances where the crowd will give fuel to the fire. One instance is when the crowd is on the player's side because of an event that was unfavorable for the player. When this happens, the player can use the crowd as a positive energy to pump themselves up. But when the crowd is on the player's side, the player must be careful not to get over-excited by the immense fire from the crowd. Use the energy from the crowd as fuel for energy to get back at the opponent, but the player must not get carried away emotionally and make judgmental mistakes. When the crowd is against the player for any reason, the negative energy can help the player by feeding off of the negative energy and turning them against the crowd. Once the crowd's fire has been put out, the player's fire will burn even stronger. The player must know that the crowd has no side and the crowd cannot change the outcome of victory to defeat and defeat to victory. Once the war has ended in victory, the crowd will respect the player as long as the player does not take any negative actions towards the crowd.

The environmental factors cannot be changed by the player. Being angry at the environment can be pointless, but by carefully studying the cause of the anger, it can help the player handle the environmental factors to use them against the opponent. For example, if the player is getting angry because of the wind, the player can use the anger as a trigger to start noticing the wind direction to use the wind favorably. Linesmen and chair umpires are also environmental factors that can't be changed since they should not be calling lines with emotion or by taking sides. They do make mistakes and by questioning a call and getting a feel for the crowd to judge if the call was indeed a mistake and was unfavorable to the player, this can help turn the crowd against the opponent and positive energy can be fed from the crowd. Arguing with the umpire will only feed negative energy to oneself and it should only be used if the player is desperate for any kind of energy.

b) Possible developments with fire attacks

"In attacking with fire, one should be prepared to meet five possible developments:

(1) When fire breaks out inside to enemy's camp, respond at once with an attack from the outside.

(2) If there is an outbreak of fire, but the enemy's soldiers remain quiet, bide your time and do not attack.

(3) When the force of the flames has reached its height, follow it up with an attack, if that is practicable; if not, stay where you are.

(4) If it is possible to make an assault with fire from the outside, do not wait for it to break out within, but deliver your attack at a favorable moment.

(5) When you start a fire, be to windward of it. Do not attack against the wind. A wind that rises in the daytime lasts long, but a night breeze soon falls.

In every army, the five developments connected with fire must be known, the movements of the stars calculated, and a watch kept for the proper days. Hence those who use fire as an aid to the attack show intelligence; those who use water as an aid to the attack gain an accession of strength. By means of water, an enemy may be intercepted, but not robbed of all his belongings."

[Translation]

This section explains how to react to the fire based on the enemy's actions. Although emotional and mental attacks can be from outside, most of the fire starts internally. When the opponent is angry at themselves (internal fire), the plan is to attack them at the source of the anger. When players get angry, it's usually because of their own actions or problems. Be it technical or tactical, the player must watch and listen to the opponent's actions to attack what it is that is irritating them.

When the opponent is starting to get irritated but calm, do not attack right away. In warfare, if a fire was started from within but the enemy is still calm, it can mean that the enemy has already anticipated the use of fire and has already evacuated or they can be waiting to launch a surprise attack to counter the fire attack. If the opponent lets their anger out to wake themselves up, it is best not to provoke them and feed more energy for them to use it against the player. Watch their actions to wait until the fire is fully developed.

When the fire is violently burning in the enemy's camp, the situation has to be watched to see how it will further develop. It's not practical to go into the enemy's camp when the fire is too heavy and it is best to surround the enemy rather than to go into the flames. When the opponent is raging violently, it is best to leave them to self-destruct. Feeding the flames by provoking them might result in opposite consequences to the player's intentions, especially when the fire was towards other factors besides the player. The player should not step in and catch fire themselves.

When the opponent is known or seems to be mentally vulnerable, they can be attacked by using different methods. There are various ways to attack an opponent with dirty tactics, but the details of how to use them will not be discussed in this book. By attacking the opponent mentally, even if the opponent has the upper hand in the score, the player can cut off the opponent's momentum and shift the momentum towards the player.

When attacking with fire, the direction of the wind is very important to keep the flames away from the allies. When the direction of the wind is ignored, the fire can catch on to the allies and cause more damage to the allies than to the enemies. In a tennis match, the player has to judge if the use of emotional attacks will be advantageous by sensing the momentum of the match. As it is with all tactics and strategies, timing of the attack is very important to shift the momentum back to the player. Provoking and taunting the opponent might not be so advantageous if it's not used at the right time or if the opponent likes to get provoked and it gives the opponent a reason to defeat the player.

c) A kingdom that has once been destroyed can never come again into being

> "Unhappy is the fate of one who tries to win his battles and succeed in his attacks without cultivating the spirit of enterprise; for the result is waste of time and general stagnation. Hence the saying: The enlightened ruler lays his plans well ahead; the good general cultivates his resources. Move not unless you see an advantage; use not your troops unless there is something to be gained; fight not unless the position is critical. No ruler should put troops into the field merely to gratify his own spleen; no general should fight a battle simply out of pique. If it is to your advantage, make a forward move; if not, stay where you are. Anger may in time change to gladness; vexation may be succeeded by content. But a kingdom that has once been destroyed can never come again into being; nor can the dead ever be brought back to life. Hence the enlightened ruler is heedful, and the good general full of caution. This is the way to keep a country at peace and an army intact."

[Translation]

Not only is it difficult to control and use fire as a weapon, the power of fire can potentially destroy everything that needs to be conquered in war and leave nothing to be conquered. Using anger to control your opponents can be a powerful tool if used properly, but improper use of anger will destroy any respect that the opponents and other players had for the player and it will be difficult to earn respect from them once again. Be cautious about using direct mental attacks towards the opponents.

Although, what goes on inside the court is left on the court, it is not the case with offensive emotional attacks.

XIII.

INTELLIGENCE AND ESPIONAGE (用間)

This is the last chapter in the book *The Art of War*. This final chapter deals with how spies should be used in warfare. Since Sun Tzu emphasized the importance of knowing the enemy beforehand, this chapter explains how information can be obtained through the use of people involved in the affairs of the state. Although this chapter's content can be applied in the initial calculations or in the earlier chapters, this chapter was sorted to be in the last chapter because of how warfare is based on deception. One must not trust anyone easily and the use of information from others can lead to devastating consequences if the information is not properly filtered by the person that is receiving information. Although you should trust members of your own team, the information from others should be used very carefully.

Secrets of the methods of the generals and the tacticians were guarded as if they were their lives. Rackets, equipment, strategy, player's tendencies, and almost everything has to be well protected by the player and coach. In professional tennis, the method of giving false information is rarely used. Coaches and players from different teams usually have mutual respect for one another and are willing to share information with one another. Parents in junior and lower level tournaments usually receives lots of new information from others and it is quite difficult for them to filter some of the information they receive. The parents must rely on their wisdom, judgment, and experience in order for them to decide which information can be used to benefit the team.

a) Getting information from others

> *"Raising a host of a hundred thousand men and marching them great distances entails heavy loss on the people and a drain on the resources of the State. The daily expenditure will amount to a thousand ounces of silver. There will be commotion at home and abroad, and men will drop down exhausted on the highways. As many as seven hundred thousand families will be impeded in their labor. Hostile armies may face each other for years, striving for the victory which is decided in a single day. This being so, to remain in ignorance of the enemy's condition simply because one grudges the outlay of a hundred ounces of silver in honors and emoluments, is the height of inhumanity. One who acts thus is no leader of men, no present help to his sovereign, no master of victory. Thus, what enables the wise sovereign and the good general to strike and conquer, and achieve things beyond the reach of ordinary*

> men, is foreknowledge. Now this foreknowledge cannot be elicited from spirits; it cannot be obtained inductively from experience, nor by any deductive calculation. Knowledge of the enemy's dispositions can only be obtained from other men."

[Translation]

This section emphasizes the importance of prior knowledge. Knowing the enemies beforehand is a prerequisite for all operations. Sun Tzu is explaining how information should be obtained by use of other people. There are limitations to obtaining critical information by observing a nation externally. The importance to obtaining information about the enemy has already been mentioned in the Weaknesses and Strengths chapter and Movement of the Army chapter. The problem with obtaining information with spies beforehand is with filtering the information that is received. The player's parents will be bombarded with information by other coaches and parents and it's easy to get influenced by the information they receive. The parents must be broad-minded, bold, and generous to be able to judge clearly what is beneficial and what is not. It is best to discuss the information with the player's coach and again judge from information given by two different people or parties.

The coach can ask various people and receive information about his or her player's opponent. Whether it be a player, coach, or the parents, the coach must ask people that have firsthand experience with the opponent. Once the information is received, the coach must also watch the opponent beforehand to match the information that was received to the foreknowledge the coach has about the opponent and also look for any new information that the coach can get from watching the opponent. Once the information is concluded to be accurate, the coach can pass on the information to the player and they can discuss what the player can expect during match play. If the information is not definite, then it is best to not mention it to the player.

For the player, the information that is given from the coach or others must not be fully relied on. The coach will probably let the player know the tendencies of the opponent and some patterns the opponent will use in certain situations. They can keep the information in mind, but must not fully rely on it because of the changing variations during a match. As mentioned in the Variation and Adaptation chapter, the player must be ready to adapt to the changes instead of having a set way of playing a match.

b) Information from different types of people

"Hence the use of spies, of whom there are five classes:

(1) Birthplace spies;

(2) Inward spies

(3) Converted spies;

(4) Doomed spies;

(5) Surviving spies.

When these five kinds of spy are all at word, none can discover the secret system. This is called "divine manipulation of the threads." It is the sovereign's most precious faculty.

Having birthplace spies means employing the services of the person who is originated from a certain district. Having inward spies, making use of officials of the enemy. Having converted spies, getting hold of the enemy's spies and using them for our own purposes. Having doomed spies, doing certain things openly for purposes of deception, and allowing our spies to know of them and report them to the enemy. Surviving spies, finally, are those who bring back news from the enemy's camp.

Hence it is that which none in the whole army are more intimate relations to be maintained than with spies. None should be more liberally rewarded. In no other business should greater secrecy be preserved. Spies cannot be usefully employed without a certain intuitive sagacity. They cannot be properly managed without benevolence and straightforwardness.

Without subtle ingenuity of mind, one cannot make certain of the truth of their reports. Be subtle! Be subtle! And use your spies for every kind of business. If a secret piece of news is divulged by a spy before the time is ripe, he must be put to death together with the man to whom the secret was told."

[Translation]

Gathering information about an opponent can be critical to winning matches consistently. Keeping a track record and tendencies of other players can help the player prepare for what is to come in the match. It can also give the player a tremendous boost to their fighting spirit if the information is about an opponent's injury or loss of motivation during certain phases of their travels.

The types of spies in ancient times can be interpreted into the following:

(1) Birthplace spies – Parents, coaches, or players from a specific region

Parents, coaches, or players that are from a specific region or country can be of help when the player is traveling to their birth country or region. They can give various information about the region and the tendencies of the players in that specific region. The various information about a region can be the conditions of a region discussed in Chapter 7: Military Maneuvers, Section c.

(2) Inward spies – friends of the coach that are coaches for other players

Inward spies can be interpreted as other players' coaches that the player's coach is close to. They can give information about a player if their player has played that specific player recently or in the past. The coaches that are familiar with each other share information about players other than theirs quite well since they will need information in the future from the person who is in need of the information.

(3) Converted spies – parents and players that do not like your opponent

Parents and players share information if they do not care so much about the opponent that the player is going to be playing. They can have grudges against a certain player for a bad loss or cheating, and it is very easy to get information from the parents and players that despise your opponent. Since there's always some kind of rivalry between players, it is important to treat other parents, coaches, and players with the utmost respect and become allies with them rather than turning everyone into your enemy.

(4) Doomed spies – friends of both sides

Some players deliver false information to their friends. The friends then inform their friends about the player. Although some information might be true, if the information is exaggerated, then the people on the receiving end can be manipulated. An example of this would be talking about a light injury or discomfort a player might have to a friend, but exaggerating the injury or discomfort can have their friends carry the message to their friends. The word gets around fast and the words can get to the player's opponent if the information is shared with the right crowd.

(5) Surviving spies – the information brought back by the friend of both

sides

The friend that has carried the exaggerated information can get back to the player and talk about the readiness or the state of the opponent by talking to them casually. The information from others is talked about casually and it is not to give someone an edge because the person with the information is friends to both of the players playing against each other. By purposely and plainly asking the weaknesses and the other player's tendencies to people that are not close, it can lead to wariness from other players. Also the parents, coaches, or players that question can become a target themselves.

The main reason this chapter is the last chapter can be assumed because of the following phrase, *"Spies cannot be usefully employed without a certain intuitive sagacity."* In order for the parents, coaches, or players to use the information given by others, they must be able to interpret the information accurately. Knowing the exact intentions of the other's words can vary a great deal. Sage-like minds who can read the intentions of others and have true knowledge in tennis can help their players gain an edge in their matches or guide them through their tennis career. If any information is taken lightly, then it can endanger the team's both short- and long-term goals.

c) Befriending other nation's officers and spies

"Whether the object be to crush an army, to storm a city, or to assassinate an individual, it is always necessary to begin by finding out the names of the attendants, the aides-de-camp, and deer-keepers and sentries of the general in command. Our spies must be commissioned to ascertain these. The enemy's spies who have come to spy on us must be sought out, tempted with bribes, led away and comfortably housed. Thus they will become converted spies and available for our service. It is through the information brought by the converted spy that we are able to acquire and employ birthplace and inward spies. It is owing to his information, again, that we can cause the doomed spy to carry false tidings to the enemy. Lastly, it is by his information that the surviving spy can be used on appointed occasions. The end and aim of spying in all its five varieties is knowledge of the enemy; and this knowledge can only be derived, in the first instance, from the converted spy. Hence it is essential that the converted spy be treated with the utmost liberality.

Of old, the rise of the Yin dynasty was due to I Chih who had served under Hsia. Likewise, the rise of the Chou dynasty was due to Lu Ya who had served under the Yin. Hence it is only the enlightened ruler and the wise general who will use the highest intelligence of the army for purposes of spying and thereby they achieve great results. Spies are a most important element in military tactics, because on them depends an army's ability to move."

[Translation]

This explains the importance of converted spies in military tactics. The converted spies are treated with the utmost kindness because they provide important information about the enemy. Not only is it a moral duty to be kind to other people; it is best to remain peaceful and friendly to other parents, coaches, and players for the benefit of the team. Any friends of the team can be their eyes and ears for the team to provide useful information. It is impossible for one team to know everything and the friends of the team will not only provide information about other players; they can provide useful information about other factors to help the player make better decisions on their route to be the best that they can be. It is best to treat others with genuine and sincere kindness rather than pretending to be friendly.

EPILOGUE:
AFTER THE PROFESSIONAL TENNIS LIFE

"I DON'T WANT MY KIDS TO PLAY PROFESSIONAL TENNIS"

Unlike members of other professions, even if they have made it to the top and have succeeded in reaching their goals as professional tennis players, most tennis players do not want their kids to play professional tennis. The top pros know exactly what it takes to make it to the top and know how tough and lonely the professional life can get. Even if a player has made enough money to support their children playing tennis, it takes much time and effort from the parents. It's not that they will disapprove and prevent their children from playing tennis, but they will probably wish for them to avoid the professional route. Think of war veterans that have seen, survived, and won many battles. It is one thing to be in the battle themselves but another to see their child go through so much suffering caused by the battles regardless of what the reason.

This book was not written to discourage players and parents but to present a clear view of what is needed and what has to be done in order for an individual to be successful when trying to become a pro tennis player. Unity of the team, financial status, discipline, mindset, deception, strategy (i.e., the laws of defense and direct attack) are all needed to support the player's athleticism and talent.

Made in the USA
Middletown, DE
25 February 2019